INTRODUCTION OF INSURANCE MARKET

SURJEET KUMAR

Introduction

of

Insurance Market

Asst. Prof. Surjeet Kumar
(B. Com. M. Com., MH-SET, TS-SET, PGDIBO,
Completed PCC Examination of CA.)

Also Useful for

1. Along with BBA and BBA(IB) this book is useful for Certificate, Diploma and Undergraduate courses offered by various state and central universities.
2. A complete Textbook for everyone interested in learning about Insurance Markets.
3. This book is worth reading for academicians, researchers, and corporate leaders as well.

License Notes

Disclaimer:-

“We've packed this book with the latest insights, along with some history thrown in for good measure! Of course, no book is perfect. If you spot something amiss, drop us a line! We'd love to hear from you and keep this book top-notch for future readers.”

e-mail: hmrspoetry@gmail.com

Dedicated to

Almighty Lord

Acknowledgment

First and foremost, I express my gratitude to the Supreme God, who inspires me to write with ease and creativity. I cannot imagine the completion of this book without the blessings of my parents, support of wife and cooperation of Ajit. I express my gratitude to all my teachers, friends, well-wishers, and critics whose feedback provides me with subjects to write even more. How can I forget to express my gratitude to my readers and students, whose suggestions act as fuel for my writing.

Table of Contents

Chapter 1

Insurance Industry Overview and Market Structure

1.1 Evolution and Growth of the Insurance Market in India

1.1.1 Historical Background: Pre- and Post-Independence Era

1.1.2 Nationalization and the Emergence of LIC and GIC

1.1.3 Liberalization and Entry of Private Players (Post-2000)

1.1.4 Current Trends in Market Growth and Penetration

1.2 Structure of the Indian Insurance Sector

1.2.1 Segmentation: Life Insurance vs. General (Non-life) Insurance

1.2.2 Health Insurance and Microinsurance Segments

1.2.3 Reinsurance and Specialized Insurance Products

1.3 Major Market Participants

1.3.1 Classification: Public Sector vs. Private Sector Insurers

1.3.2 Life Insurance Companies

1.3.3 Non-Life and Health Insurance Companies

1.3.4 Role of Agents, Brokers, and Corporate Agents

1.4 Major Players and Market Leaders

1.4.1 LIC (Life Insurance Corporation of India): Market Share and Reach

1.4.2 GIC (General Insurance Corporation): Role as Reinsurer

1.4.3 Major Private Players:

HDFC Life

ICICI Lombard

SBI Life, Max Life, Bajaj Allianz, etc.

1.4.4 Comparative Analysis: Public vs. Private Performance

1.5 Global Insurance Markets and Trends

1.5.1 Overview of Global Insurance Landscape

1.5.2 Emerging Markets vs. Developed Markets

1.1 Evolution and Growth of the Insurance Market in India

The insurance market in India has evolved through a long journey of transformation, influenced by historical events, regulatory reforms, and economic changes. Initially introduced during the colonial era, insurance was primarily designed to serve European interests in British India. However, over time, the sector adapted to the socio-economic needs of independent India and continues to expand in the contemporary digital age.

The Indian insurance industry has undergone four significant phases: the unregulated colonial period, the era of nationalization post-independence, the liberalization wave in the early 2000s, and the current phase marked by technology and inclusive growth. The earliest insurance companies catered to select communities with limited reach and oversight. Post-independence, the government nationalized both life and general insurance segments to protect policyholders and align insurance with national development goals.

The formation of the Life Insurance Corporation (LIC) in 1956 and General Insurance Corporation (GIC) in 1972 centralized and stabilized the sector. However, the lack of competition limited innovation and efficiency. The economic reforms of the 1990s led to the opening up of the insurance sector to private and foreign players through the establishment of the Insurance Regulatory and Development Authority of India (IRDAI) in 1999. This brought about significant changes, including customer-centric product designs, digital platforms, and improved service standards.

Currently, India's insurance industry is experiencing steady growth, supported by increasing financial literacy, government welfare schemes, and a youthful population. The emergence of InsurTech, use of data analytics, and mobile-based policy distribution have further widened market access. However, challenges remain in terms of deepening penetration in rural areas and ensuring long-term sustainability.

Overall, the evolution of India's insurance market reflects a balance between public welfare objectives and market efficiency, with significant potential for future expansion.

1.1.1 Historical Background: Pre- and Post-Independence Era

The history of insurance in India dates back to the early 19th century, with the establishment of the Oriental Life Insurance Company in 1818 in Kolkata. This and other early ventures were largely managed by British firms to serve European citizens residing in India. Indian nationals were often subject to discriminatory premium rates and policy conditions. The sector lacked regulation, and most companies operated with limited accountability and inconsistent underwriting practices.

The pre-independence period saw the emergence of several Indian-owned insurance companies, such as Bombay Mutual Life Assurance Society (1870), which was the first to offer life insurance to Indians. Despite these developments, the insurance market remained fragmented, with limited oversight and frequent insolvencies, which weakened public trust. Post-independence, the government viewed insurance as a critical tool for financial security and national development. Concerns about unethical practices and the collapse of private insurers led to legislative intervention. In 1956, the life insurance industry was nationalized through the Life Insurance Corporation Act, resulting in the formation of LIC, which absorbed over 245 companies into a single, state-controlled entity. This move aimed to standardize practices, protect policyholders, and mobilize resources for national planning. Similarly, the general insurance sector underwent nationalization in 1972 with the passage of the General Insurance Business (Nationalisation) Act. The government established the General Insurance Corporation (GIC) along with four subsidiaries to manage non-life insurance operations. These steps marked a shift towards state monopoly in the insurance sector, ensuring stability but also limiting competition.

In essence, the historical trajectory of the insurance market before and after independence reflects India's broader economic priorities—transitioning from colonial exploitation to welfare-oriented nation-building through state control. This foundation set the stage for future reforms, especially during the liberalization era.

1.1.2 Nationalization and the Emergence of LIC and GIC

Following India's independence in 1947, the government recognized the strategic importance of the insurance industry in safeguarding public interest and channeling financial resources toward national development. Concerns over mismanagement, fraud, and insolvency in the fragmented private insurance market prompted the need for centralized regulation and control. This led to the nationalization of the life insurance and general insurance sectors in two key phases.

In 1956, the Government of India nationalized the life insurance business through the enactment of the Life Insurance Corporation Act. More than 245 private life insurance companies were merged to form the Life Insurance Corporation of India (LIC). LIC was entrusted with the twin responsibilities of spreading life insurance awareness across the country and mobilizing long-term savings for economic development. It rapidly expanded its operations, introduced standardized policies, and built a strong distribution network even in rural areas.

Similarly, in 1972, the general insurance business was nationalized under the General Insurance Business (Nationalisation) Act. The General Insurance Corporation of India (GIC) was created as a holding company, and four public sector companies—National Insurance, New India Assurance, Oriental Insurance, and United India Insurance—were formed as its subsidiaries. These companies handled all forms of non-life insurance such as motor, health, fire, and marine insurance.

The nationalization of insurance aimed to ensure equitable access, policyholder protection, and social security. It also helped channel insurance premiums into infrastructure and industrial investments. However, the state monopoly also led to operational inefficiencies, limited innovation, and poor customer service in the long run.

Nevertheless, this period laid a strong institutional foundation for the industry and enhanced public trust in insurance. It also set the stage for the eventual opening up of the sector during the liberalization era of the 1990s.

1.1.3 Liberalization and Entry of Private Players (Post-2000)

The liberalization of the Indian economy in the early 1990s marked a major shift in government policy from state-led development to market-driven reforms. The insurance sector, which had operated as a government monopoly for decades, was identified as a potential area for reform due to its untapped market potential, low penetration, and need for modernization.

In 1993, the Government of India appointed the Malhotra Committee to evaluate the functioning of the insurance sector and recommend changes. The committee advocated for greater competition, improved efficiency, and the establishment of an independent regulatory body. Acting on these recommendations, the government passed the Insurance Regulatory and

Development Authority Act, 1999, leading to the creation of the Insurance Regulatory and Development Authority of India (IRDAI) in 2000.

The IRDAI opened the doors for private sector companies and foreign joint ventures (with a cap on foreign direct investment). Major private players such as ICICI Prudential, HDFC Life, Bajaj Allianz, and SBI Life entered the market, bringing in advanced technology, innovative products, and customer-centric services. The entry of private insurers also fostered competition, which led to better pricing, increased product variety, and improved service quality.

This liberalized environment also encouraged the use of digital platforms, bancassurance, and third-party distribution channels, making insurance more accessible. Additionally, specialized insurance products like unit-linked insurance plans (ULIPs), microinsurance, and customized health plans were introduced to cater to diverse market needs.

Despite rapid growth, the market faced challenges such as mis-selling, low financial literacy, and the need for stronger regulation. IRDAI played a crucial role in addressing these issues by implementing guidelines to protect policyholders and ensure fair competition.

The liberalization of the insurance sector transformed it from a state-dominated system to a dynamic, competitive marketplace, thereby contributing significantly to financial inclusion and economic development in India.

1.1.4 Current Trends in Market Growth and Penetration

In recent years, the Indian insurance industry has experienced dynamic growth, driven by regulatory reforms, digital transformation, and increasing public awareness. Despite a historically low insurance penetration rate compared to global standards, the sector is now witnessing promising trends that indicate a shift toward broader market inclusion and expansion.

Insurance penetration, measured as the ratio of premium to GDP, has steadily improved due to proactive policy measures and rising financial literacy. Initiatives like Pradhan Mantri Jeevan Jyoti Bima Yojana (PMJJBY), Pradhan Mantri Suraksha Bima Yojana (PMSBY), and Ayushman Bharat have brought millions of previously uninsured individuals into the formal insurance network, particularly in rural and low-income segments.

Technology adoption is another defining trend. The rise of InsurTech firms and digital platforms has revolutionized policy issuance, claims processing, customer service, and fraud detection. Artificial intelligence (AI), big data analytics, and mobile apps are being leveraged to personalize offerings, reduce costs, and enhance operational efficiency. Online comparison portals have empowered consumers to make informed choices based on transparency and convenience.

Private insurers continue to lead innovation in product development, offering flexible, customer-centric plans such as health top-ups, critical illness covers, and unit-linked insurance plans (ULIPs). Additionally, microinsurance and usage-based policies are expanding access for underserved populations and gig economy workers.

Distribution channels have also diversified. Apart from traditional agents, insurers now use bancassurance, digital marketing, corporate brokers, and online aggregators to reach customers. This multichannel approach enhances reach and improves policy servicing.

Despite progress, challenges persist in terms of insurance awareness, trust deficits, and complexity of products. Regulatory bodies like the IRDAI continue to focus on simplifying policies, promoting transparency, and enhancing grievance redressal mechanisms.

Overall, the Indian insurance market is undergoing a transformation, with growing penetration, customer engagement, and technological integration shaping its future trajectory.

1.2 Structure of the Indian Insurance Sector

The Indian insurance sector is a diverse and evolving landscape, designed to offer financial protection to individuals, businesses, and communities against various types of risks. The structure of this sector is governed by the Insurance Regulatory and Development Authority of India (IRDAI), which oversees all insurance activities and licenses public and private players. The market is broadly classified into life insurance and general (non-life) insurance, with additional sub-segments such as health insurance, microinsurance, and reinsurance. India's insurance industry includes a mix of public sector undertakings like the Life Insurance Corporation (LIC) and four major general insurers, alongside several private sector companies and foreign joint ventures. This multi-operator model ensures a competitive environment and enhances service standards, product variety, and customer access across urban and rural regions.

1.2.1 Segmentation: Life Insurance vs. General (Non-life) Insurance

This classification is based on the type of risk covered and the nature of the insurance contract. While both forms of insurance aim to provide financial protection, they differ significantly in purpose, policy duration, benefits, and the events that trigger a claim. Understanding the distinction between these two categories is essential for policyholders, insurers, and students of insurance studies, as it helps in identifying the appropriate risk management solutions for individuals and organizations. Below are the key points of difference between life and general insurance:

i. Purpose:

Life insurance is primarily designed to provide financial protection to the family or dependents of the insured in the event of the insured's death. It also serves as a long-term financial planning tool, often offering savings, investment, and retirement benefits. In contrast, general insurance, also known as non-life insurance, is intended to cover financial losses arising from unforeseen events such as accidents, theft, fire, illness, or natural disasters. It does not offer any savings or investment component; its role is purely protective.

ii. Duration of Policy:

Life insurance policies are typically long-term in nature. Depending on the product, the duration can range from 10 years to the entire lifetime of the insured. Some policies also continue into retirement and pay out upon maturity. On the other hand, general insurance policies are short-term contracts, usually valid for one year, and must be renewed annually to maintain coverage.

iii. Claim Payment:

In life insurance, the claim is paid either on the death of the insured (in the case of term insurance) or on policy maturity (for endowment or ULIP plans). It provides a guaranteed sum assured to the nominee or policyholder. In general insurance, the claim is payable only if a covered risk or event actually occurs, such as hospitalization, a car accident, or property damage. There is no maturity benefit if no claim is made.

iv. Value and Return:

Life insurance often provides financial returns to the policyholder, either through bonuses, profit-sharing, or investment-linked returns, depending on the policy type. General insurance offers no return on the premium paid unless a claim is made. The premium serves only to protect against specified risks during the policy period.

v. Examples of Products:

Examples of life insurance products include term insurance, endowment plans, whole life policies, pension plans, and Unit Linked Insurance Plans (ULIPs). General insurance covers a wide range of products such as motor vehicle insurance, health insurance, fire and property insurance, marine insurance, and travel insurance.

1.2.2 Health Insurance and Microinsurance Segments

As the Indian insurance sector expands, specialized segments such as health insurance and microinsurance have emerged as critical tools for enhancing financial protection and social inclusion. These segments cater to specific needs—health-related risks and low-income population groups—thereby playing a vital role in improving national well-being and insurance penetration.

Health Insurance

Health insurance is one of the fastest-growing segments within the general insurance category. It provides financial coverage for medical expenses arising from illness, injury, hospitalization, and sometimes outpatient treatments. Depending on the plan, coverage may include pre- and post-hospitalization, daycare procedures, ambulance services, and critical illness treatment.

The demand for health insurance has increased due to rising healthcare costs, changing lifestyles, and heightened awareness—especially after the COVID-19 pandemic. Both public and private insurers offer individual, family floater, group, and senior citizen health plans. Major health insurers include Star Health, Niva Bupa, Care Health, and general insurers such as ICICI Lombard and New India Assurance.

Government-sponsored schemes such as Ayushman Bharat – Pradhan Mantri Jan Arogya Yojana (PM-JAY) aim to provide free health coverage to economically weaker sections, covering over 500 million beneficiaries.

Microinsurance

Microinsurance refers to low-cost insurance products tailored for low-income individuals, particularly in rural and informal sectors. These products provide protection against specific risks such as death, disability, health emergencies, crop failure, or loss of livestock, at affordable premiums and simplified terms.

Microinsurance plays a crucial role in financial inclusion by providing a safety net to vulnerable populations. Government schemes like Pradhan Mantri Suraksha Bima Yojana (PMSBY) and Pradhan Mantri Jeevan Jyoti Bima Yojana (PMJJBY) offer accidental and life insurance to eligible citizens for nominal premiums.

1.2.3 Reinsurance and Specialized Insurance Products

As the Indian insurance market matures and diversifies, segments like reinsurance and specialized insurance products have become integral to the structure and stability of the industry. These components support risk management at a systemic level and enable insurers to offer customized solutions for complex or emerging risks.

i. Reinsurance

Reinsurance is a form of insurance purchased by insurance companies themselves. It allows insurers to transfer a portion of their risk to another company—known as the reinsurer—in exchange for a premium. This mechanism provides financial stability, enhances the insurer's capacity to underwrite high-value or large-volume policies, and protects them against catastrophic losses.

In India, General Insurance Corporation of India (GIC Re) is the primary domestic reinsurer and also operates internationally. The liberalization of the sector has allowed global reinsurers like Swiss Re, Munich Re, and SCOR to set up operations in India. Reinsurance helps insurers manage risks more efficiently and promotes healthy underwriting practices across the industry.

ii. Specialized Insurance Products

Specialized insurance refers to customized insurance solutions that cover specific or non-standard risks not fully addressed by conventional policies. These products are tailored for particular industries, professions, or risk categories and are gaining popularity as economic activities diversify and evolve.

Examples of specialized insurance products include:

Crop Insurance (e.g., under Pradhan Mantri Fasal Bima Yojana)
Cyber Risk Insurance for data breaches and digital threats
Credit and Trade Insurance for business receivables
Event and Film Insurance for production-related risks
Pet Insurance and Livestock Insurance in rural segments
These niche offerings are essential for supporting economic sectors like agriculture, technology, exports, and entertainment, while also fostering innovation in product design and risk coverage.

1.3 Major Market Participants

The Indian insurance market is comprised of a diverse group of participants operating under the regulatory framework established by the Insurance Regulatory and Development Authority of India (IRDAI). These participants include life insurance companies, general (non-life) insurance companies, standalone health insurers, reinsurance companies, and other intermediaries such as agents, brokers, and aggregators. The market operates through both public and private sector institutions, ensuring a competitive and inclusive insurance environment.

1.3.1 Classification: Public Sector vs. Private Sector Insurers

The Indian insurance industry operates through two broad categories of market participants: public sector insurers and private sector insurers. Both categories are regulated by the Insurance Regulatory and Development Authority of India (IRDAI), which ensures fairness, transparency, and solvency across the sector. This classification is based on ownership and capital structure, and each category plays a distinct role in developing the insurance ecosystem.

Firstly, in terms of ownership, public sector insurers are wholly or majority-owned by the Government of India. These include companies like LIC, GIC Re, and four general insurance firms (New India Assurance, Oriental, National, and United India Insurance). In contrast, private sector insurers are owned by private Indian promoters, often in joint ventures with foreign insurance companies. These include firms like HDFC Life, ICICI Lombard, and Star Health, operating under IRDAI regulations.

Secondly, their market approach varies significantly. Public sector insurers traditionally focus on social objectives such as financial inclusion and rural outreach. Their priorities include implementing government schemes and covering low-income populations. Private insurers, on the other hand, operate with a more commercial focus, emphasizing profitability, customer retention, and competitive positioning in urban and semi-urban markets.

Thirdly, operational efficiency and service delivery tend to differ. Private insurers have been more agile in adopting digital technologies, improving customer service, and streamlining claims processing. Public sector companies, while reliable, often face bureaucratic delays and slower service turnaround due to legacy systems and administrative hierarchies.

Fourthly, product innovation is more prominent in the private sector, which actively designs flexible, customizable, and technology-integrated insurance solutions. Private players have introduced offerings like ULIPs, online term plans, wellness-linked health policies, and app-based services. In contrast, public insurers generally offer more standardized products with limited customization.

Lastly, in terms of geographic presence, public sector insurers have an extensive reach across rural and remote areas, owing to their long-standing presence and wide agency network. Private insurers are gradually expanding their footprint, but their primary concentration remains in urban and economically active regions.

1.3.2 Life Insurance Companies

Life insurance companies are specialized financial institutions that offer long-term protection and savings products designed to provide financial security to individuals and their families. These companies play a vital role in mobilizing long-term savings, promoting financial discipline, and supporting national capital formation through investments in infrastructure and government securities.

In India, life insurance companies operate under the regulatory supervision of the Insurance Regulatory and Development Authority of India (IRDAI). They offer a range of products including term insurance, endowment plans, whole life policies, Unit Linked Insurance Plans (ULIPs), pension plans, and child education plans. These products are designed not only to cover the risk of premature death but also to support life-stage financial goals such as retirement planning and wealth accumulation.

Public Sector Life Insurer

The most prominent and the only public sector life insurance company in India is the Life Insurance Corporation of India (LIC), established in 1956 after the nationalization of over 245 private insurers. LIC has built a legacy of trust and extensive reach, particularly in rural and semi-urban areas. It enjoys a dominant market share and a vast agency network that enables it to serve millions of policyholders across the country.

Private Sector Life Insurers

Following liberalization in 2000, several private companies entered the life insurance space, many of them as joint ventures with foreign insurers. These companies have introduced innovative, technology-driven, and customer-friendly insurance solutions. Leading private life insurers include:

HDFC Life Insurance

ICICI Prudential Life Insurance

SBI Life Insurance

Max Life Insurance

Bajaj Allianz Life Insurance

Private players have significantly contributed to product diversification, service enhancement, and digital adoption in the life insurance domain.

1.3.3 Non-Life and Health Insurance Companies

on-life insurance companies, also known as general insurance companies, provide coverage against risks and financial losses that do not pertain to human life. These include risks related to property damage, vehicle accidents, health emergencies, travel disruptions, liability claims, and more. Non-life insurance policies are typically short-term contracts, usually for a year, and must be renewed periodically. These companies play a vital role in safeguarding individuals, businesses, and assets against unforeseen events.

The general insurance sector in India is regulated by the Insurance Regulatory and Development Authority of India (IRDAI). It comprises both public sector insurers, which have historically catered to mass-market needs, and private sector players, who have driven innovation and improved customer service.

Public Sector General Insurers

India has four major public sector general insurance companies:

New India Assurance Company Limited

United India Insurance Company Limited

National Insurance Company Limited

Oriental Insurance Company Limited

These companies have a strong legacy and widespread presence across the country. They are actively involved in implementing government-sponsored schemes such as the Pradhan Mantri Fasal Bima Yojana (crop insurance) and Ayushman Bharat (health insurance).

Private Sector General Insurers

Post-liberalization, private companies entered the market with improved service quality, technology integration, and customer-centric products. Leading private general insurers include:

ICICI Lombard General Insurance

Bajaj Allianz General Insurance

HDFC ERGO General Insurance

Tata AIG General Insurance

These companies offer a wide variety of policies tailored to individual, corporate, and industrial needs.

Standalone Health Insurance Companies

In response to rising healthcare costs and increasing demand for specialized coverage, standalone health insurance companies have emerged. They focus exclusively on health-related products such as hospitalization cover, critical illness plans, and wellness services. Key players include:

Star Health and Allied Insurance

Niva Bupa Health Insurance

Care Health Insurance

1.3.4 Role of Agents, Brokers, and Corporate Agents

In the Indian insurance industry, intermediaries such as agents, brokers, and corporate agents play a critical role in bridging the gap between insurance companies and customers. They are responsible for promoting insurance awareness, assisting in product selection, ensuring proper documentation, and facilitating claims. These intermediaries are licensed and regulated by the Insurance Regulatory and Development Authority of India (IRDAI) to ensure ethical conduct and professional standards.

A. Roles of Insurance Agents

i. Prospecting and Policy Promotion

Insurance agents play a frontline role in identifying potential customers and introducing them to various insurance offerings. They actively search for prospects through personal networks, door-to-door visits, community outreach, or referrals. Their role involves creating awareness about the importance of insurance, especially among individuals with little prior exposure to financial products. Agents act as brand ambassadors for the insurance company and contribute significantly to expanding its customer base.

ii. Client Needs Assessment

Agents are trained to understand and analyze a client's specific needs based on factors such as age, income, dependents, and financial goals. They then recommend suitable products—like term plans for pure protection or ULIPs for long-term savings. This personalized approach enhances customer satisfaction and ensures that the policy purchased is aligned with the client's risk profile. A well-assessed recommendation often leads to better policy retention and claim experience.

iii. Assisting in Policy Application

The policy application process can be complex, involving detailed forms, document verification, and sometimes medical tests. Insurance agents guide clients through each step, ensuring that all required information is accurately filled in and that compliance requirements are met. They clarify policy terms, explain exclusions, and help the applicant make informed choices. Their assistance reduces errors and delays, resulting in quicker policy issuance.

iv. Premium Collection and Renewal Reminders

Agents often assist in collecting the initial premium and may also help customers set up payment reminders or renewal arrangements. Regular follow-up ensures that policies remain in force and do not lapse due to missed payments. Agents also inform customers about any changes in premium structure, coverage, or benefits during renewal. By maintaining this ongoing relationship, agents help build trust and long-term client engagement.

v. Claims Assistance and Servicing

One of the most crucial responsibilities of an insurance agent is to assist the policyholder or nominee during the claim process. Agents help collect and submit the necessary documents and track the claim's status with the insurer. Their support is especially important in emotionally sensitive situations like death claims. Prompt and empathetic service during this phase enhances the company's credibility and improves customer satisfaction.

B. Roles of Insurance Brokers

i. Comparative Product Analysis

Insurance brokers are independent professionals who provide unbiased advice to clients by comparing multiple insurance products. They assess offerings from various insurers in terms of coverage, premium, exclusions, and benefits. This helps clients choose the most suitable policy from a broad range of available options. Unlike agents, who represent a single company, brokers offer greater product flexibility and transparency.

ii. Risk Assessment and Advisory

Brokers conduct a thorough assessment of the client's risk exposure—whether personal, professional, or business-related. For corporate clients, this includes analyzing operations, liabilities, property values, and workforce-related risks. Based on their findings, brokers recommend appropriate insurance solutions tailored to specific risk profiles. Their expertise is critical in designing customized policies for complex sectors like manufacturing, logistics, healthcare, or IT.

iii. Negotiation with Insurers

Since brokers act on behalf of the client, they negotiate directly with insurers to obtain better terms, lower premiums, and broader coverage. Their knowledge of market conditions and insurer practices gives them leverage in discussions. This role is particularly useful when clients require non-standard or high-value policies. The broker ensures that the client receives maximum value for the premium paid.

iv. Policy Administration and Support

Once a policy is issued, brokers continue to support their clients by helping with endorsements, changes in coverage, or renewals. They maintain records, send reminders for policy expiries, and manage documentation throughout the policy lifecycle. This reduces the administrative burden on clients and ensures continuous coverage. They also help clarify any doubts that arise during the term of the policy.

v. Claims Management and Advocacy

One of the most valuable roles brokers play is assisting in the claims process. They help gather documentation, liaise with insurers, and follow up to ensure timely claim settlement. In case of disputes, they represent the client's interests and help resolve issues through negotiation or escalation. Their involvement often results in quicker, more favorable claim outcomes for the policyholder.

C. Roles of Corporate Agents

i. Insurance Distribution through Existing Channels

Corporate agents are organizations—such as banks, NBFCs, or co-operatives—that distribute insurance using their existing infrastructure. For example, a bank acting as a corporate agent may offer life, health, or general insurance to customers during routine banking transactions. This model leverages the trust and convenience of existing relationships to improve insurance penetration. Customers benefit from easy access to insurance products without needing to visit a separate office.

ii. Cross-Selling and Upselling

Corporate agents often bundle insurance products with other financial services like loans, credit cards, or fixed deposits. For example, personal accident insurance may be offered with a savings account, or home insurance with a mortgage loan. This method helps increase insurance uptake with minimal additional effort. Cross-selling also provides value-added protection for customers while increasing revenue streams for the corporate agent.

iii. Policy Servicing Infrastructure

These institutions typically have trained personnel and digital systems that allow for issuing policies, collecting premiums, and servicing customer queries. Customers can access policy details, pay premiums, or file claims at the same counters where they conduct other transactions. This integrated servicing model improves efficiency and enhances customer satisfaction. It also reduces the cost of operations for the insurer.

iv. Digital Integration and Efficiency

Many corporate agents—especially banks and fintech firms—integrate insurance offerings into mobile apps, internet banking, and ATMs. This digital interface enables customers to purchase or manage insurance policies 24/7, improving convenience. Digital platforms also allow for instant policy issuance, tracking, and support. This technology-driven approach contributes to faster, more transparent service delivery.

v. Compliance and Reporting

As licensed intermediaries, corporate agents must adhere to IRDAI's strict guidelines on ethical conduct, transparency, and recordkeeping. They are responsible for maintaining proper sales documentation, disclosing commissions, and ensuring that customers are well informed. Regular audits and reporting to the regulator help maintain accountability. Compliance ensures that the interests of both the customer and insurer are protected.

1.4 Major Players and Market Leaders

India's insurance sector comprises a mix of public sector giants and private players, each contributing uniquely to the overall growth and stability of the market. Among the most prominent institutions are the Life Insurance Corporation of India (LIC) and the General Insurance Corporation of India (GIC). These two organizations play pivotal roles, with LIC dominating the life insurance sector and GIC being the sole reinsurer in the Indian market.

1.4.1 LIC (Life Insurance Corporation of India): Market Share and Reach

The Life Insurance Corporation of India (LIC), established in 1956 through the nationalization of over 240 private insurers, is the largest life insurance company in India. It holds a dominant position in the Indian life insurance market, both in terms of premium collection and the number of policies under management. As a public sector undertaking, LIC operates under the regulatory framework of the Insurance Regulatory and Development Authority of India (IRDAI) and the Ministry of Finance.

LIC commands over 60% of the market share in life insurance, even after the liberalization of the insurance sector, which saw the entry of numerous private players. Its widespread presence includes over 2,000 branches, 1.5 lakh employees, and an extensive network of over 12 lakh agents. This deep-rooted infrastructure allows LIC to penetrate both urban and rural markets, ensuring financial inclusion and insurance accessibility across the country.

The corporation offers a diverse portfolio of products, including term insurance, endowment plans, money-back policies, pension schemes, and unit-linked insurance plans (ULIPs). LIC is also instrumental in mobilizing long-term savings for national development projects and infrastructure funding. Its reputation for trust, claim settlement efficiency, and wide reach makes it a market leader in the Indian life insurance domain.

1.4.2 GIC (General Insurance Corporation): Role as Reinsurer

The General Insurance Corporation of India (GIC Re) serves as the national reinsurer and plays a critical role in supporting the Indian insurance market. Established in 1972 as a public sector company, GIC Re was originally the holding company for four public sector general insurance companies. However, after the restructuring of the insurance sector in 2000, GIC was designated as the sole national reinsurer in India.

Reinsurance is a mechanism that allows insurance companies to transfer a portion of their risk portfolios to another company—in this case, GIC Re—thus enhancing their capacity to underwrite large or high-risk policies. GIC Re's primary function is to provide this risk-sharing support to Indian insurers, enabling them to manage exposures related to natural catastrophes, industrial hazards, aviation, marine, and other specialized sectors.

GIC Re has a strong presence not only in India but also globally. It operates in over 160 countries and has established branches or subsidiaries in countries such as the UK, South Africa, Malaysia, and the UAE. Its global footprint allows it to diversify risk geographically and remain financially resilient.

Moreover, GIC Re is instrumental in maintaining stability within the Indian insurance market by supporting new product innovation, ensuring solvency margins of insurers, and promoting international best practices. It works in close coordination with IRDAI and contributes to policy research and data analytics that benefit the broader industry.

As a reinsurer, GIC Re plays a strategic role in strengthening the financial backbone of the insurance sector, making it one of the most significant players in the ecosystem.

1.4.3 Major Private Players:

The liberalization of India's insurance sector in 2000 opened the doors for private participation, leading to the emergence of several dynamic and customer-centric insurance companies. Over the past two decades, private insurers have significantly contributed to increasing insurance penetration, product innovation, and customer service standards. Some of the leading private players in the Indian insurance market include HDFC Life, ICICI Lombard, SBI Life, Max Life, and Bajaj Allianz.

HDFC Life is one of the top-performing private life insurers, known for its wide range of term and savings plans, strong digital presence, and efficient claim settlement ratio. The company has adopted a hybrid distribution strategy involving bancassurance (especially through HDFC Bank), agents, and online channels.

ICICI Lombard leads the non-life insurance segment among private players, offering diverse products such as health, motor, travel, and corporate insurance. The company is widely recognized for its tech-driven approach, fast claim processing, and customer engagement through mobile apps and portals.

SBI Life, backed by the State Bank of India, has a significant presence due to the bank's extensive network, offering affordable life insurance products to both urban and rural customers. Max Life focuses on long-term savings and protection plans, and has been consistently ranked high in customer satisfaction. Bajaj Allianz, with its strong brand and operational efficiency, operates in both life and non-life segments and is praised for innovation and customer service.

These companies have brought in global expertise, capital, and modern management practices. Through multi-channel distribution, competitive pricing, and tailored products, private insurers have successfully attracted younger, tech-savvy customers and contributed to the rapid evolution of the Indian insurance landscape.

1.4.4 Comparative Analysis: Public vs. Private Performance

The Indian insurance sector is marked by a healthy mix of public and private entities, each with distinct operational philosophies and market strategies. A comparative analysis highlights the strengths and weaknesses of both segments, offering insights into their performance, outreach, and impact on the industry.

i. Market Share and Reach: Public sector insurers like LIC (life) and New India Assurance (general) still command the majority market share, primarily due to their legacy presence, trust factor, and wide rural reach. In contrast, private players have rapidly expanded in urban and semi-urban areas, leveraging technology and strategic partnerships to gain market traction.

ii. Innovation and Technology: Private insurers are often more agile and adaptive when it comes to innovation. They have introduced app-based services, AI-powered claim processing, and customer analytics. Public sector entities, while modernizing gradually, often face bureaucratic delays and legacy system challenges.

iii. Product Variety and Customization: Private insurers offer highly tailored products targeting different life stages, income groups, and risk profiles. Public insurers tend to focus on traditional offerings, though they are beginning to expand their product ranges to compete.

iv. Customer Service and Claim Settlement: While LIC enjoys a high claim settlement ratio, private insurers like Max Life and HDFC Life have also matched or exceeded these benchmarks in recent years. However, private firms generally outperform public ones in terms of customer responsiveness and service quality due to more efficient internal processes.

v. Profitability and Efficiency: Private insurers tend to operate with better cost-efficiency and higher profitability margins. Their focus on selective underwriting and tech-driven operations contributes to leaner business models, unlike public firms which carry social responsibilities that sometimes affect their bottom line.

1.5 Global Insurance Markets and Trends

The global insurance market has undergone significant transformation in recent decades, shaped by economic shifts, technological innovation, changing demographics, and evolving risk landscapes. While the core objective of insurance—managing risk and providing financial protection—remains unchanged, how insurance is delivered, structured, and consumed has changed drastically. Understanding global insurance markets and trends is essential for analyzing India's position and for learning from international best practices.

1.5.1 Overview of Global Insurance Landscape

The global insurance industry is broadly divided into life insurance and non-life (general) insurance sectors. As of recent global reports, total global insurance premiums have crossed USD 7 trillion, with the largest contributions coming from the United States, China, Japan, and European Union countries. The U.S. remains the largest single market, while China is rapidly expanding and is projected to become the largest by mid-2030s.

The global landscape is highly diversified. Developed economies tend to have high insurance penetration (measured as a percentage of GDP), while emerging markets show strong growth potential due to under-penetration and rising middle-class income. Innovations like InsurTech, digital underwriting, cyber risk insurance, and parametric insurance are reshaping the way insurance operates worldwide. Additionally, global risks such as climate change, pandemics, and geopolitical conflicts are creating new categories of coverage and risk management solutions.

Reinsurance, cross-border partnerships, and multinational insurers play a key role in stabilizing markets and distributing global risk. Regulatory harmonization through organizations such as the International Association of Insurance Supervisors (IAIS) is also influencing the global structure. Overall, the insurance landscape is becoming more interconnected and technology-driven.

1.5.2 Emerging Markets vs. Developed Markets

The global insurance industry reflects sharp contrasts between developed and emerging markets in terms of maturity, innovation, regulatory sophistication, and customer behavior. Developed markets such as the United States, United Kingdom, Germany, Japan, and Canada have high insurance penetration, well-established regulatory frameworks, and mature customer bases. Insurers in these markets focus on advanced underwriting, digital transformation, and new product innovation like retirement planning, long-term care insurance, and climate risk coverage. The challenges in these regions include market saturation, aging populations, and pressure on profitability due to low interest rates.

Emerging markets—including India, Brazil, Indonesia, Vietnam, and African economies—are characterized by low insurance penetration, young and growing populations, and expanding middle classes. These markets offer immense potential for growth. Insurance awareness, financial literacy, and digital access are rising rapidly, driven by mobile technology and government initiatives. Products are typically simpler and more affordable, often distributed via bancassurance, mobile platforms, and microinsurance models.

The difference also lies in regulatory maturity. Developed markets have highly structured solvency regimes, while emerging markets are evolving toward risk-based capital norms. However, emerging markets often outperform in terms of adaptability, leapfrogging traditional systems and adopting digital-first models.

1.5.3 Global Players and Their Influence

Several global insurance companies exert significant influence over the international insurance landscape due to their scale, expertise, and multinational presence. Notable among them are Allianz SE (Germany), AXA (France), MetLife (USA), Prudential plc (UK/Asia), Ping An (China), and Swiss Re and Munich Re (global reinsurers).

These players operate in dozens of countries and offer a broad range of insurance services—life, health, property, casualty, and specialty insurance. Their influence lies not only in market share but also in product innovation, capital strength, and thought leadership. Many lead global research in risk management, catastrophe modeling, ESG (Environmental, Social, Governance) integration, and digital transformation.

Global reinsurers such as Swiss Re and Munich Re play a critical role in supporting local insurers across the world, including in India, by providing reinsurance capacity and advanced actuarial models. These global players are also key investors in technology startups (InsurTech), promoting automation, AI, blockchain, and big data in insurance.

In addition, global insurers help shape regulatory and ethical standards through participation in international forums. Their lobbying efforts, influence in capital markets, and risk pooling abilities impact global pricing trends and risk distribution.

In India, many of these players operate through joint ventures—for example, ICICI Prudential (with Prudential plc) or HDFC Life (with Standard Life Aberdeen)—bringing global practices into the local market. These collaborations contribute to improving underwriting standards, digital services, and customer education in the Indian insurance ecosystem.

1.5.4 Lessons for India from Global Practices

India's insurance sector can draw multiple valuable lessons from international markets to improve coverage, customer experience, and financial sustainability.

First, product diversification and customization seen in developed markets can be emulated. Indian insurers can offer more personalized policies using data analytics and behavioral modeling, as done in countries like the U.S. and UK. Products linked to retirement, wellness, and climate change coverage are relatively underdeveloped in India and can be adapted from global models.

Second, technological integration is a key area. Many global insurers use AI, machine learning, and IoT (Internet of Things) to streamline underwriting, claims management, and fraud detection. India can replicate these technologies, especially in health and crop insurance segments, where accurate data can improve service and reduce loss ratios.

Third, regulatory agility is crucial. India can learn from solvency frameworks and consumer protection standards of markets like the EU (Solvency II regime) and the U.S. Risk-based capital norms, embedded value disclosures, and digital grievance redressal mechanisms can improve transparency and investor confidence.

Fourth, microinsurance and inclusive models from countries such as Kenya (M-TIBA) and Bangladesh (Grameen schemes) offer insights into reaching underserved populations. While India has schemes like PMFBY and PMJJBY, a stronger partnership with private insurers and digital platforms can improve reach and efficiency.

Finally, environmental and social governance (ESG) frameworks adopted by leading global insurers can help Indian firms align with global climate goals and attract ESG-focused investors.

By studying and adapting global best practices, India can accelerate its transition to a more inclusive, resilient, and modern insurance industry.

1.6 Regulatory Framework: Role of IRDAI

The Indian insurance sector operates under a structured and evolving regulatory environment aimed at ensuring financial stability, consumer protection, and market efficiency. The Insurance Regulatory and Development Authority of India (IRDAI) is the apex statutory body entrusted with overseeing and regulating the insurance industry. Established post-liberalization, IRDAI plays a pivotal role in ensuring that insurance companies act in the interest of policyholders, maintain solvency, and contribute to the sector's orderly growth. Through licensing, supervision, policy formulation, and grievance handling, IRDAI provides a robust institutional framework that promotes innovation while safeguarding public interest.

1.6.1 Establishment and Objectives of IRDAI

The IRDAI was established in 1999 under the Insurance Regulatory and Development Authority Act, 1999, as part of the government's effort to liberalize and modernize the insurance sector. Before its formation, the insurance industry was largely state-controlled with minimal competition. IRDAI was created as an autonomous body to regulate, promote, and ensure the orderly growth of both life and non-life insurance in India.

The primary objectives of IRDAI include:

i. Protecting the interests of policyholders.

ii. Ensuring fair competition and financial soundness of insurers.

iii. Promoting efficiency and innovation in the insurance market.

iv. Encouraging penetration in underserved areas, particularly rural and social sectors.

v. Regulating insurance intermediaries such as agents, brokers, and third-party administrators.

IRDAI functions independently but reports to the Ministry of Finance, ensuring transparency and accountability. It issues guidelines, circulars, and notifications that are binding on insurers and intermediaries. With its proactive role, IRDAI serves as both a regulator and a facilitator—striking a balance between safeguarding consumers and enabling market development.

1.6.2 Licensing and Regulation of Insurers

One of the core responsibilities of IRDAI is to license and regulate insurance companies operating in India. Before any insurer—whether in life, general, or health insurance—can start operations, it must obtain a license from IRDAI after fulfilling prescribed eligibility norms, including capital requirements, foreign equity limits, and fit-and-proper criteria for promoters. The licensing process involves scrutiny of business plans, solvency margins, financial soundness, and management structures. IRDAI also licenses insurance intermediaries, such as agents, brokers, web aggregators, and third-party administrators (TPAs), ensuring they meet professional standards and ethical benchmarks.

IRDAI mandates strict regulatory compliance, including:

i. Maintaining minimum solvency margins.

ii. Submitting periodic financial and actuarial reports.

iii. Ensuring corporate governance practices.

iv. Filing products and obtaining approvals before market launch.

v. Adhering to pricing and underwriting guidelines, especially in regulated sectors like health and motor insurance.

Additionally, IRDAI monitors foreign direct investment (FDI) compliance and sets norms for joint ventures between Indian and foreign insurers. Any violation of these norms can attract penalties, suspension, or cancellation of licenses.

Through this rigorous licensing and regulatory mechanism, IRDAI ensures that only competent and financially sound players operate in the Indian insurance space, thereby promoting a stable and competitive market.

1.6.3 Policyholder Protection and Grievance Redressal

Protecting the interests of policyholders is a central mandate of IRDAI. The regulator has established comprehensive frameworks to ensure transparency, fairness, and accountability in insurer-customer interactions. It mandates all insurers to treat policyholders with dignity and deliver on contractual promises without delay or ambiguity.

IRDAI has issued a Policyholder Protection Regulations, which outlines:

i. Timely issuance of policy documents.

ii. Transparent disclosure of terms and conditions.

iii. Free-look period provisions for cancellation.

iv. Timely and fair settlement of claims.

v. Guidelines on mis-selling, advertising, and customer communication.

For grievance redressal, IRDAI requires each insurer to establish a Grievance Redressal Mechanism (GRM) with a dedicated officer and online complaint tracking. Additionally, IRDAI operates the Integrated Grievance Management System (IGMS)—a centralized platform where policyholders can register complaints online and track resolution progress. If unresolved at the company level, complaints can be escalated to IRDAI's Consumer Affairs Department or further addressed by the Insurance Ombudsman.

IRDAI also conducts periodic audits and surveys to assess customer satisfaction and enforce compliance. Penalties are imposed on insurers for unfair practices or delays in claim settlements.

This multi-layered protection framework significantly boosts customer trust and market credibility, making insurance more approachable and accountable to Indian citizens.

1.6.4 Impact of IRDAI on Market Stability and Transparency

IRDAI has played a transformative role in shaping a transparent, stable, and inclusive insurance ecosystem in India. Its policies have helped shift the sector from a monopolistic setup to a competitive, innovation-driven market with over 60 licensed insurers, multiple distribution channels, and rising penetration levels.

By enforcing solvency norms, capital adequacy requirements, and prudent underwriting guidelines, IRDAI ensures that insurance companies remain financially sound, even during economic downturns or calamities. This contributes significantly to market stability, as seen during the COVID-19 pandemic, when IRDAI swiftly introduced new guidelines for health coverage, premium deferrals, and digital servicing.

In terms of transparency, IRDAI mandates detailed disclosures by insurers related to claim settlement ratios, grievance handling, financial statements, and investment patterns. This helps customers make informed decisions and promotes ethical competition. It also fosters investor confidence and ensures regulatory compliance.

Furthermore, IRDAI has been instrumental in promoting digital adoption, financial inclusion, and social sector insurance through initiatives like:

Sandbox regulations for InsurTech innovation.

Mandating rural and social sector obligations.

Promoting microinsurance and government schemes like PMJJBY and PMFBY.

In essence, IRDAI acts as the cornerstone of the Indian insurance sector—balancing regulatory oversight with developmental vision. Its efforts ensure that the market remains robust, fair, and aligned with both global best practices and national welfare goals.

For Quick Revision

1.1 Evolution and Growth of the Insurance Market in India

1.1.1 Historical Background: Pre- and Post-Independence Era

- Insurance in India began in the early 19th century (Oriental Life Insurance, 1818).
- Unregulated growth and malpractices in pre-independence era.
- Post-independence: push for structured and regulated insurance sector.

1.1.2 Nationalization and the Emergence of LIC and GIC

- Life insurance nationalized in 1956: formation of LIC.
- General insurance nationalized in 1972: creation of GIC.
- Nationalization brought trust, scale, and reach to rural India.

1.1.3 Liberalization and Entry of Private Players (Post-2000)

- Insurance sector opened to private players in 2000.
- Formation of IRDAI as a regulator.
- Entry of private and foreign joint ventures increased competition and product innovation.

1.1.4 Current Trends in Market Growth and Penetration

- Growth driven by rising awareness, technology, and financial inclusion.
- Insurance penetration still low compared to global average.
- Focus on digitalization, customer-centric products, and rural outreach.

1.2 Structure of the Indian Insurance Sector

1.2.1 Segmentation: Life Insurance vs. General (Non-life) Insurance

- Life insurance: death benefit, savings, retirement (e.g., LIC, HDFC Life).
- General insurance: motor, property, travel, fire, marine (e.g., ICICI Lombard).

1.2.2 Health Insurance and Microinsurance Segments

- Health insurance: hospitalization, critical illness, COVID-19 coverage.
- Microinsurance: low-premium products for low-income groups.

1.2.3 Reinsurance and Specialized Insurance Products

- Reinsurance: risk-sharing among insurers (GIC Re is key player).
- Specialized products: crop insurance, cyber insurance, climate risk coverage.

1.3 Major Market Participants

1.3.1 Classification: Public Sector vs. Private Sector Insurers

- Public: LIC, New India Assurance, etc.
- Private: HDFC Life, ICICI Lombard, Max Bupa, etc.

1.3.2 Life Insurance Companies

- Offer term plans, endowment, ULIPs, annuities.
- LIC dominates with the largest market share.

1.3.3 Non-Life and Health Insurance Companies

- Cover general risks like motor, fire, and health.
- Include Star Health, Niva Bupa, and public firms like United India Insurance.

1.3.4 Role of Agents, Brokers, and Corporate Agents

- Agents: individual sales representatives.
- Brokers: licensed intermediaries offering client-centric advice.
- Corporate agents: banks or institutions selling policies from multiple insurers.

1.4 Major Players and Market Leaders

1.4.1 LIC (Life Insurance Corporation of India): Market Share and Reach

- Over 60% life insurance market share.
- Massive rural presence, trusted brand, government-backed.

1.4.2 GIC (General Insurance Corporation): Role as Reinsurer

- India's sole reinsurer (until recently).
- Provides reinsurance support to Indian and foreign insurers.

1.4.3 Major Private Players

- HDFC Life, ICICI Lombard, SBI Life, Max Life, Bajaj Allianz, etc.
- Known for product innovation, digital servicing, and urban market focus.

1.4.4 Comparative Analysis: Public vs. Private Performance

- Public: wider reach, government schemes.
- Private: customer service, tech adoption, flexible products.
- Growing collaboration between public and private players.

1.5 Global Insurance Markets and Trends

1.5.1 Overview of Global Insurance Landscape

- Mature markets: USA, UK, Japan, Germany.

- Emerging markets: China, India, Brazil are rapidly expanding.

1.5.2 Emerging Markets vs. Developed Markets

- Developed markets have high penetration, product maturity.
- Emerging markets show faster growth, tech adoption, low coverage base.

1.5.3 Global Players and Their Influence

- Global insurers like AXA, Allianz, Prudential operate in India via JVs.
- Influence local product standards and risk management practices.

1.5.4 Lessons for India from Global Practices

- Need for deeper penetration, better claims experience, digital focus.
- Importance of customer education, product transparency, and risk-based pricing.

1.6 Regulatory Framework: Role of IRDAI

1.6.1 Establishment and Objectives of IRDAI

- Formed in 1999 under IRDA Act.
- Regulates, promotes, and ensures orderly insurance growth.

1.6.2 Licensing and Regulation of Insurers

- Grants licenses to life, general, health, and reinsurance companies.
- Sets rules for capital adequacy, solvency, and governance.

1.6.3 Policyholder Protection and Grievance Redressal

- Enforces fair practices, timely claim settlement.
- Maintains IRDAI grievance portal and consumer helpline.

1.6.4 Impact of IRDAI on Market Stability and Transparency

- Ensures insurer solvency, standardization of products.
- Promotes healthy competition, tech adoption, and innovation.

Test Your Knowledge

2-Marks Questions

1. Define insurance in the context of economic development.
2. What was the state of the Indian insurance sector before independence?
3. Mention two key changes brought by the nationalization of the insurance sector.
4. Name any two major private insurance players that entered the market post-2000.
5. Differentiate between life insurance and general insurance in brief.
6. What do you mean by microinsurance?
7. Write any two features of health insurance in India.
8. List two roles of insurance brokers.
9. What is the full form of LIC and GIC?
10. Who regulates the insurance market in India?
11. State any two objectives of IRDAI.
12. Mention two key functions of reinsurance.
13. What is meant by insurance market penetration?
14. List two benefits of liberalization in the insurance sector.
15. Name any two global insurance companies.
16. Give two points of difference between public and private insurers.
17. What are specialized insurance products? Give examples.
18. Mention any two grievances redressal measures by IRDAI.
19. Define the term "policyholder protection."
20. Name two types of agents in the insurance sector.
21. What role does GIC play in the Indian insurance system?
22. Mention any two emerging global trends in the insurance industry.
23. State one major difference between developed and emerging insurance markets.
24. Who are corporate agents in the insurance distribution system?
25. Write any two reasons for the growth of private insurers post-liberalization.

5-Marks Questions

1. Explain the key developments in the Indian insurance sector before and after independence.
2. Discuss the impact of nationalization on the Indian insurance industry with a focus on LIC and GIC.

3. Analyze the role of liberalization in transforming the Indian insurance landscape since 2000.
4. Compare the life insurance and general insurance segments in India with suitable examples.
5. Evaluate the importance of microinsurance and health insurance in the Indian context.
6. Explain the role and functioning of reinsurance in risk management within the insurance industry.
7. Differentiate between public and private sector insurers based on ownership, reach, and performance.
8. Identify and explain the contributions of major players such as LIC, HDFC Life, and ICICI Lombard to the Indian insurance market.
9. Analyze the influence of global insurance players on the Indian insurance ecosystem.
10. Assess the lessons India can learn from global best practices in insurance.
11. Explain how IRDAI contributes to ensuring transparency and policyholder protection.
12. Discuss the structure and segmentation of the Indian insurance sector.
13. Illustrate the role of intermediaries like agents, brokers, and corporate agents in insurance sales and distribution.
14. Compare the market performance of public vs. private players using recent trends and statistics.
15. Examine the major trends in the global insurance markets and how they may affect the Indian industry.

Chapter 2

Market Products, Distribution and Customer Segments

2.1 Insurance Product Segmentation

2.1.1 Life Insurance Products:

Term Plans

Endowment Plans

Unit Linked Insurance Plans (ULIPs)

2.1.2 General Insurance Products:

Health Insurance

Motor Insurance

Crop Insurance

Fire and Marine Insurance

2.2 Emerging Insurance Products

2.2.1 Cyber Insurance

2.2.2 Travel Insurance

2.2.3 Microinsurance for Low-Income Groups

2.2.4 Pandemic and Climate Risk Insurance (optional addition)

2.3 Distribution Channels in Insurance

2.3.1 Agency System

Individual Agents

Corporate Agents

Training and Licensing

2.3.2 Bancassurance

Tie-ups between Banks and Insurers

Models and Revenue Sharing

2.3.3 Digital and Online Platforms

Role of Aggregators (e.g., Policy Bazaar, Coverfox)

Direct-to-Customer (D2C) Sales and Mobile Apps

Chatbots and AI in Policy Recommendations

2.1 Insurance Product Segmentation

Insurance products are broadly classified into life insurance and non-life insurance (general insurance), with each category tailored to address specific financial needs and risks. Within life insurance, various products serve different purposes such as income protection, savings, investment, and retirement planning. Product segmentation enables insurers to design offerings suited to customers' age, income, risk appetite, and financial goals. In this section, we explore the key life insurance products that dominate the Indian market.

2.1.1 Life Insurance Products:

Life insurance products primarily offer financial protection against the risk of premature death, along with saving and investment benefits in some variants. The major types of life insurance plans include:

A. Term Insurance Plans

Term plans are the most basic and affordable form of life insurance. These plans provide pure risk coverage, meaning the insurer pays the sum assured only if the policyholder dies during the policy term. If the insured survives the term, no maturity benefit is paid (except in Return of Premium variants).

Features:

i. Low premium and high sum assured.

ii. Fixed policy tenure (e.g., 10, 20, 30 years).

iii. Ideal for income protection and family security.

iv. No savings or investment component.

Term plans are particularly suitable for young earners, parents with dependent children, or individuals with loans and liabilities. Riders like critical illness, accidental death, and disability can enhance coverage.

B. Endowment Plans

Endowment plans combine insurance protection with savings. A portion of the premium goes toward life cover, while the rest is invested by the insurer. If the policyholder survives the policy term, a maturity benefit is paid. In case of death, the sum assured plus bonuses (if any) are paid to the nominee.

Features:

i. Fixed sum assured and maturity date.

ii. Guaranteed returns along with potential bonuses.

iii. Moderate premium amounts.

iv. Encourages long-term financial discipline.

Endowment policies are ideal for conservative investors seeking assured returns and life cover. They are often used for goals such as children's education, marriage, or retirement corpus.

C. Unit Linked Insurance Plans (ULIPs)

ULIPs are market-linked insurance products that offer both life insurance and investment opportunities. A part of the premium goes toward providing life cover, while the remaining is invested in equity, debt, or hybrid funds, depending on the policyholder’s choice.

Features:

i. Dual benefit of insurance and wealth creation.

ii. Investment risk borne by the policyholder.

iii. Flexible fund-switching options.

iv. Lock-in period of 5 years.

ULIPs are suitable for financially literate individuals with medium to high-risk appetite and long-term investment goals. Over time, ULIPs have become more customer-friendly with lower charges, transparent fund performance, and online tracking.

2.1.2 General Insurance Products:

General insurance, also known as non-life insurance, provides coverage against specific financial losses arising from unforeseen events such as illness, accidents, property damage, or natural disasters. Unlike life insurance, general insurance policies are usually short-term contracts and do not offer maturity benefits. These products are crucial for risk management in personal, commercial, and agricultural contexts. The major types of general insurance products in India include health insurance, motor insurance, crop insurance, and fire and marine insurance.

A. Health Insurance

Health insurance policies provide financial protection against medical expenses incurred due to illness, injury, or hospitalization. With rising healthcare costs, health insurance has become a critical component of personal financial planning.

Features:

i. Covers hospitalization expenses, surgeries, diagnostics, and sometimes OPD treatments.

ii. Available as individual, family floater, senior citizen, and group policies.

iii. May include add-ons such as critical illness cover, maternity benefits, and day-care procedures.

iv. Cashless treatment is often available through a network of partner hospitals.

Health insurance promotes access to quality healthcare while reducing the financial burden during medical emergencies. It is offered by both public and private insurers and is increasingly being integrated with wellness and preventive care programs.

B. Motor Insurance

Motor insurance is mandatory under the Motor Vehicles Act, 1988, for all vehicles operating on Indian roads. It offers financial protection against damage to the vehicle, third-party liabilities, and theft.

Features:

i. Classified into third-party insurance (mandatory) and comprehensive insurance (optional).

ii. Covers damages to the insured vehicle, third-party injury or property damage, and personal accident benefits.

iii. Add-ons include zero depreciation, engine protection, roadside assistance, etc.

iv. Policyholders must renew the policy annually to remain compliant.

Motor insurance is one of the largest segments in the general insurance industry, supported by growing vehicle ownership and regulatory enforcement.

C. Crop Insurance

Crop insurance protects farmers against financial losses due to crop failure caused by natural calamities, pests, diseases, or adverse weather conditions. It plays a vital role in supporting the rural economy and stabilizing agricultural income.

Features:

i. Covers sowing risk, mid-season adversity, and post-harvest losses.
ii. Offered through schemes like the Pradhan Mantri Fasal Bima Yojana (PMFBY).
iii. Premiums are subsidized by the government to ensure affordability for farmers.
iv. Claims are based on yield estimates or weather index data, depending on the policy type.

Crop insurance helps reduce farmers' dependency on informal credit and mitigates the financial impact of unpredictable farming conditions, fostering agricultural resilience.

D. Fire and Marine Insurance

Fire and Marine Insurance are two fundamental forms of general insurance that provide essential protection for property and goods. These types of insurance are particularly important for businesses and industries, as they safeguard against potential losses arising from damage to assets and goods in transit. Both insurance types serve distinct but critical functions in risk management and economic continuity.

I. Fire Insurance

Fire insurance provides coverage against loss or damage to property caused by fire and related perils. It is typically availed by individuals, businesses, and industries to protect physical assets such as buildings, machinery, furniture, stock, and other valuables.

Features:

Covers not only fire but also lightning, explosion, implosion, storm, cyclone, and damage due to water used for extinguishing the fire.

i. Policies can be issued for residential, commercial, and industrial properties.
ii. Claims are settled on either a market value or reinstatement value basis.
iii. Optional add-ons include coverage for loss of profits due to business interruption (known as consequential loss insurance).

Fire insurance is vital for ensuring business continuity, especially in sectors where even a minor fire incident can lead to significant operational and financial losses.

II. Marine Insurance

Marine insurance covers the loss or damage of goods, ships, cargo, and other movable property during transit—whether by sea, air, road, or rail. It is indispensable in both domestic and international trade.

Marine insurance is classified into:

Marine Hull Insurance: Covers ships and vessels against damage due to accidents, collision, piracy, or natural disasters.

Marine Cargo Insurance: Covers goods in transit against risks like theft, damage, or non-delivery.

Features:

i. Ensures risk mitigation in global trade and logistics.

ii. Policies may be issued per voyage, annually, or as open policies for frequent shipments.

iii. Required by banks and lenders as a risk cover for financed shipments.

2.2 Emerging Insurance Products

The insurance industry is constantly evolving to meet new types of risks that arise from technological advancements, demographic shifts, and global challenges. In recent years, the emergence of new product categories—such as cyber insurance, travel insurance, microinsurance, and pandemic or climate risk insurance—reflects a proactive response to emerging vulnerabilities and societal needs. These products demonstrate the sector's adaptability and the growing role of insurance in personal and global risk management.

2.2.1 Cyber Insurance

Cyber insurance is a relatively new but rapidly growing segment that provides coverage against risks arising from cyberattacks, data breaches, and digital fraud. With the increasing digitalization of businesses and dependence on online platforms, cyber threats have become a significant concern.

Features:

i. Covers financial losses due to hacking, malware attacks, data theft, ransomware, and denial of service (DoS) attacks.

ii. Includes coverage for legal expenses, data restoration, business interruption, and reputational damage.

iii. Applicable to businesses, financial institutions, and even individuals exposed to digital risks.

iv. Risk assessment is based on IT infrastructure, cybersecurity practices, and previous incidents.

Cyber insurance plays a critical role in enterprise risk management, especially for IT firms, banks, healthcare providers, and e-commerce platforms. It also encourages better cybersecurity protocols by rewarding risk-mitigating behavior with lower premiums.

2.2.2 Travel Insurance

Travel insurance provides protection against various risks associated with domestic and international travel. It is particularly important in an era of global mobility and unpredictable travel disruptions.

Features:

i. Covers trip cancellations, medical emergencies, lost baggage, passport theft, and flight delays.

ii. Optional covers may include adventure sports injuries or COVID-19-related medical expenses.

iii. Available for individuals, families, or corporate groups, and often bundled with credit cards or tour packages.

iv. Travel policies can be short-term (per trip) or annual multi-trip.

Travel insurance ensures peace of mind for travelers by mitigating financial risk during unforeseen events abroad. It has gained prominence post-pandemic, with increasing awareness about health emergencies and travel restrictions.

2.2.3 Microinsurance for Low-Income Groups

Microinsurance refers to low-premium, low-coverage insurance products designed specifically for economically vulnerable populations. It plays a pivotal role in financial inclusion and social security for underserved communities.

Features:

i. Covers life, health, accident, crop, and livestock risks with simplified terms and quick claim processing.

ii. Premiums are highly affordable, often subsidized or linked with government welfare schemes.

iii. Distributed through self-help groups (SHGs), NGOs, microfinance institutions, and rural banks.

iv. Encourages savings, builds financial resilience, and reduces dependence on informal credit.

Examples include India's Pradhan Mantri Jeevan Jyoti Bima Yojana (PMJJBY) and Rashtriya Swasthya Bima Yojana (RSBY). Microinsurance helps uplift low-income families by protecting them from income shocks and asset erosion due to unforeseen events.

2.2.4 Pandemic and Climate Risk Insurance

In the wake of increasing global uncertainties, Pandemic and Climate Risk Insurance has emerged as a crucial innovation in the insurance industry. This product aims to provide financial protection against large-scale health crises like COVID-19 and environmental disasters resulting from climate change, such as floods, cyclones, droughts, and wildfires. Pandemic Insurance is designed to support businesses, governments, and individuals in managing the economic fallout of infectious disease outbreaks. It covers losses due to forced closures, supply chain disruptions, and workforce unavailability. These policies are particularly valuable for sectors like travel, hospitality, and retail that are vulnerable to shutdowns.

Climate Risk Insurance, on the other hand, addresses the growing frequency and severity of weather-related events. It offers compensation for property damage, agricultural losses, and business interruptions caused by climate-related hazards. Products may be customized for regions prone to specific risks, and may include parametric insurance solutions where payouts are triggered by pre-defined environmental conditions (e.g., rainfall below a threshold).

As both pandemic and climate threats intensify, such insurance products are gaining attention from policymakers, regulators, and insurers globally. They also promote climate resilience and public health preparedness, and often involve collaboration with governments or international agencies for large-scale risk pooling and affordability.

2.3 Distribution Channels in Insurance

Distribution channels are the mediums through which insurance products reach customers. These channels play a vital role in connecting insurers with prospective policyholders. The efficiency, reach, and effectiveness of these channels significantly impact customer acquisition, service, and retention. One of the most traditional and widely used channels is the Agency System.

The agency system involves individuals or organizations that act as intermediaries between the insurance company and the customer. They help sell policies, provide after-sales service, and offer personalized guidance to clients. This system is particularly prevalent in life and general insurance sectors in India.

A. Individual Agents

Individual agents are licensed professionals who represent one insurance company and work on a commission basis. They play a direct role in advising clients, explaining policy details, collecting documents, and assisting with claims. Their personal relationships and trust-building are often key to policy sales, especially in rural and semi-urban areas.

B. Corporate Agents

Corporate agents are institutions such as banks, NBFCs, microfinance institutions, or other companies that are authorized to sell insurance products. They may represent up to three insurers — one each in life, general, and health insurance. Corporate agents benefit from an existing customer base, allowing insurers to tap into broader markets more efficiently.

C. Training and Licensing

To ensure professionalism and compliance, all agents must undergo mandatory training and obtain a license from the Insurance Regulatory and Development Authority of India (IRDAI). The training covers insurance principles, product knowledge, regulatory frameworks, and ethical selling practices. Regular renewal and continuing education are also required to maintain agent status.

2.3.2 Bancassurance

Bancassurance refers to the partnership between banks and insurance companies to sell insurance products through the bank's branches and digital platforms. This channel allows insurers to leverage the bank's existing customer base, infrastructure, and trust.

A. Tie-ups between Banks and Insurers

Banks enter into formal agreements with life, general, or health insurers to distribute their products. Customers visiting the bank can get access to insurance services alongside banking. This setup provides convenience and increases insurance penetration, especially among salaried and urban customers.

B. Models and Revenue Sharing

There are several models of bancassurance, including:

Corporate Agency Model: The bank acts as a corporate agent for up to three insurers (one per category).

Referral Model: The bank refers customers to the insurer for a commission.

Joint Venture Model: The bank and insurer create a new insurance company.

Revenue is shared based on the agreement — usually, the bank receives a commission on the sale of each policy or a share of profits.

2.3.3 Digital and Online Platforms

Digital and online platforms have revolutionized the insurance distribution landscape by offering customers greater convenience, transparency, and speed. These platforms are accessible through websites, mobile apps, and social media, and they cater especially well to tech-savvy, urban populations.

A. Role of Aggregators (e.g., PolicyBazaar, Coverfox)

Insurance aggregators are online comparison platforms that bring together offerings from multiple insurers in one place. They help users:

i. Compare policies based on price, features, and coverage.

ii. Read customer reviews and expert recommendations.

iii. Purchase insurance instantly with minimal paperwork.

Platforms like PolicyBazaar and Coverfox have become trusted sources for both information and transactions, particularly in life, motor, and health insurance.

B. Direct-to-Customer (D2C) Sales and Mobile Apps

In the Direct-to-Customer (D2C) model, insurance companies sell policies directly through their official websites or mobile applications, eliminating intermediaries. This method offers:

i. Lower premiums due to reduced distribution costs.

ii. Enhanced customer control and personalization.

iii. Easy access to services like renewal, premium payment, and claim tracking.

Mobile apps also offer push notifications, reminders, and 24/7 accessibility, improving customer engagement.

C. Chatbots and AI in Policy Recommendations

Insurance firms are increasingly using Artificial Intelligence (AI) and chatbots to assist customers online. These tools:

i. Interact in real time to answer questions and recommend suitable plans.

ii. Analyze user data (age, occupation, budget, goals) to provide tailored suggestions.

iii. Improve efficiency in onboarding, underwriting, and claims settlement.

AI-driven technologies not only enhance the user experience but also enable insurers to scale operations with minimal human intervention.

2.4 Customer Segmentation and Targeting

Customer segmentation and targeting are essential strategies in the insurance industry, aimed at identifying and serving the diverse needs of different customer groups more effectively. In a market as vast and varied as India's, insurance companies cannot offer a "one-size-fits-all" solution. Instead, they must divide the overall market into smaller segments based on various characteristics such as demographics, geography, income, occupation, lifestyle, risk profile, and preferences. This enables insurers to design and promote products that are tailored to the specific requirements of each segment, enhancing customer satisfaction and business performance.

Segmentation allows insurers to better understand what customers need, how they make decisions, and what channels they prefer. For example, the insurance needs of a salaried urban professional differ vastly from those of a rural farmer or a retired senior citizen. Similarly, businesses like MSMEs and large corporates have different levels of risk exposure and require varying degrees of coverage and customization.

Targeting is the next step after segmentation, where insurers decide which customer segments they should focus on, based on market potential, profitability, and strategic goals. Effective targeting ensures that marketing and sales efforts are concentrated on high-value or high-potential customers, improving conversion rates and optimizing resource use. For instance, a health insurer may target young working professionals in urban areas with digitally delivered plans, while a general insurer may target farmers with weather-indexed crop insurance in rural zones.

Modern segmentation also incorporates behavioral and psychographic data, allowing insurers to refine their targeting using factors like digital behavior, financial goals, and lifestyle choices. Additionally, the use of data analytics, AI, and CRM systems has made it possible to track customer patterns and personalize offerings in real-time.

2.4.1 Urban vs. Rural Insurance Markets

The Indian insurance landscape is marked by a stark divide between urban and rural markets, each with its own unique needs, challenges, and distribution dynamics. Understanding this segmentation is essential for insurers seeking to expand outreach and design customer-centric products.

i. Customer Profile and Awareness

The urban insurance market consists mainly of salaried professionals, entrepreneurs, and business owners who generally have a higher level of financial literacy and awareness about insurance products. These customers understand the importance of long-term protection and financial planning. On the other hand, rural customers are often engaged in agriculture, daily wage labor, or small-scale activities. Their awareness of insurance is usually limited, and many view it as an unnecessary or unfamiliar expense rather than a safety net. As a result, insurers must conduct awareness and education drives to encourage rural participation.

ii. Product Preferences and Risk Coverage

Urban customers prefer comprehensive products that combine protection with investment, such as Unit Linked Insurance Plans (ULIPs), term insurance with riders, and full-featured health insurance. They also seek specialized coverage like home, travel, and cyber insurance. In contrast, rural customers prioritize basic risk coverage that addresses immediate livelihood concerns. Common rural products include crop insurance, livestock insurance, micro health insurance, and personal accident plans. These products are more focused on risk mitigation rather than wealth creation.

iii. Distribution Channels

In urban areas, insurers use digital channels, aggregators, corporate agents, and direct-to-customer (D2C) platforms to sell insurance. The preference for mobile apps, online portals, and chatbot-assisted purchases is growing rapidly. Rural insurance distribution, however, depends on local agents, Self-Help Groups (SHGs), cooperatives, and government-supported outreach programs. Personal interaction and trust are crucial for rural sales, often requiring face-to-face communication in the local language.

iv. Policy Design and Complexity

Urban insurance policies often come with advanced features, multiple riders, flexible premium options, and tax-saving components. Customers demand customization and are willing to compare policies online before choosing the best fit. On the other hand, rural insurance products are simple, low-cost, and standardized, with fewer options and less paperwork. The focus is on ease of understanding and minimal documentation to encourage adoption among low-literacy populations.

v. Premium Affordability and Payment Modes

Urban customers usually have the financial capacity to pay higher premiums, often opting for annual or semi-annual payments through digital methods like net banking, credit cards, or auto-debit. In contrast, rural policyholders prefer low-ticket premiums with flexible or seasonal payment schedules, such as during harvest or festival seasons. Many rural policies also depend on government subsidies or group plans to remain affordable.

2.4.2 Insurance Needs of MSMEs and Corporates

Micro, Small, and Medium Enterprises (MSMEs) and corporate entities form the backbone of the Indian economy. Together, they contribute significantly to employment, GDP, and industrial development. However, both face a variety of operational, financial, and strategic risks—ranging from asset loss to employee liabilities and cyber threats. Insurance plays a crucial role in safeguarding these businesses from unexpected disruptions and financial distress.

A. Insurance Needs of MSMEs

i. Fire and Property Insurance

MSMEs often operate from small factories, workshops, or commercial units with valuable machinery and raw materials. Fire and property insurance protects these assets from damage caused by fire, lightning, explosions, storms, or natural disasters. This coverage is vital for business continuity, especially for enterprises that cannot afford major infrastructure losses.

ii. Burglary and Theft Insurance

This insurance provides coverage against financial loss due to burglary or attempted theft of goods, cash, or equipment. MSMEs, especially those dealing with inventory or cash transactions, are vulnerable to such incidents. Having this insurance helps in securing the premises and mitigating financial setbacks from criminal activities.

iii. Group Health Insurance

Group health insurance enables MSMEs to offer medical coverage to their employees at a lower cost compared to individual plans. It improves employee satisfaction, reduces absenteeism, and increases retention. Many insurers now offer micro-group plans tailored for small enterprises with just a few employees.

iv. Workmen's Compensation Insurance

This insurance covers legal liabilities in case an employee suffers injury or death while on duty. It is especially important for MSMEs involved in manufacturing, construction, or manual labor. The policy ensures that employees (or their families) are compensated for medical costs, disability, or loss of income, as per the Workmen's Compensation Act.

v. Liability Insurance

MSMEs are increasingly exposed to third-party claims for bodily injury, property damage, or defective products. Liability insurance safeguards businesses from legal expenses and compensation payouts. It is particularly relevant for MSMEs in food processing, chemical, or consumer goods sectors.

B. Insurance Needs of Corporates

i. Directors and Officers (D&O) Liability Insurance

This insurance protects senior executives and board members against personal liability for decisions taken in their professional roles. In today's regulatory environment, directors can face lawsuits for mismanagement, non-compliance, or misleading statements. D&O insurance covers legal fees, settlement costs, and protects corporate leadership from financial damage.

ii. Cyber Liability Insurance

Corporates handle vast amounts of sensitive customer, financial, and operational data, making them targets for cyberattacks. Cyber liability insurance provides financial protection against data breaches, ransomware, system hacks, and resulting legal claims. It also helps cover the costs of investigation, reputation management, and customer notification.

iii. Keyman Insurance

This policy covers the life of a critical employee whose expertise, leadership, or public reputation significantly contributes to the business. If the key person dies or becomes disabled, the insurance payout helps the company recover losses, recruit replacements, and maintain investor confidence. It is especially relevant in founder-led or innovation-driven companies.

iv. Employee Benefits (Group Life, Gratuity, Wellness)

Corporate firms provide a comprehensive insurance package as part of employee benefits, including group term life, gratuity management, and wellness programs. These offerings promote employee well-being and serve as incentives for hiring and retention. Customized health and pension plans also enhance the employer's brand image.

v. Business Interruption Insurance

Business operations can be disrupted due to fires, natural disasters, machinery breakdown, or political unrest. Business interruption insurance compensates for lost income during the downtime and helps cover ongoing expenses like rent and salaries. It ensures that the organization can survive financially until normal operations resume.

2.4.3 Gender-Based and Age-Based Segmentation

In insurance, understanding customer demographics such as gender and age is essential for designing relevant, inclusive, and effective insurance products. Different genders and age groups face different life risks, financial responsibilities, and healthcare needs. Insurers use this segmentation to create targeted marketing strategies, price policies accurately, and offer benefits that align with the distinct needs of each segment.

A. Gender-Based Segmentation

i. Women-Centric Insurance Products

Women-specific insurance plans address unique life and health situations such as maternity, breast or cervical cancer, and gynecological treatments. These policies often come with added benefits like wellness packages, reduced waiting periods, and discounted premiums. Insurance companies have begun to introduce financial protection plans that empower women as independent policyholders, including life and retirement policies tailored for female entrepreneurs or single mothers.

ii. Lower Risk Perception and Premium Advantage

Statistically, women are considered to have longer life expectancies and safer lifestyles compared to men. As a result, women often qualify for lower premium rates in term life insurance and health insurance. This gender-based pricing helps encourage more women to buy individual insurance, increasing their financial inclusion and protection.

iii. Awareness and Financial Literacy Initiatives

To close the gender gap in insurance adoption, insurers and regulators promote women-centric financial literacy programs. These efforts include educational campaigns, community outreach, and special incentives for first-time female policyholders. Gender-sensitive marketing strategies also play a key role in building trust and engagement with women buyers, especially in rural and semi-urban areas.

B. Age-Based Segmentation

i. Young Adults (18–30 Years)

This group is generally healthy and at a low risk of illness, making them ideal candidates for low-cost term insurance and basic health plans. They are more likely to buy insurance for compliance (such as motor insurance) or tax-saving purposes. Insurers often promote starter insurance products or digital-only plans to attract young, tech-savvy buyers.

ii. Middle-Aged Individuals (30–50 Years)

This is a crucial segment for insurers as these individuals often carry major responsibilities like home loans, children's education, and aging parents. They seek comprehensive life coverage, family health insurance, and investment-linked products like ULIPs or endowment plans. Insurers offer policies with features like premium waivers, income replacement, and critical illness riders to serve this life stage.

iii. Senior Citizens (60+ Years)

Older individuals typically face higher health risks and may have limited income after retirement. Their insurance needs include senior-specific health policies, critical illness cover, and pension or annuity plans. Insurance products for this group often come with shorter waiting periods, lifetime renewability, and high sum insured options, though premiums may be higher due to age-related risk.

2.4.4 Group Insurance and Customized Products

The insurance industry today recognizes that customers are not homogenous. Individuals and organizations have unique needs based on size, income, profession, health conditions, and risk exposure. To address this diversity, insurers offer two major solutions—Group Insurance and Customized Products—which help in delivering broader access and greater relevance in insurance coverage.

A. Group Insurance

i. Concept and Benefits

Group insurance refers to a single policy that covers a defined group of people, such as employees of a company, members of a cooperative, or customers of a microfinance institution. It offers coverage at a lower premium because the risk is spread across many individuals. It is an efficient and affordable way to extend basic insurance coverage to large populations, especially in low-income or informal sectors.

ii. Types of Group Insurance

The most common forms of group insurance include:

Group term life insurance: Provides financial protection to the nominee if a group member dies during the policy term.

Group health insurance: Covers hospitalization and medical expenses for all members.

Group personal accident insurance: Offers compensation in case of accidental death or disability.

Group insurance can be voluntary or employer-funded. It is widely used by companies as part of their employee benefits program and by governments to promote social security.

iii. Accessibility and Distribution

Group insurance plays a key role in promoting financial inclusion, especially in rural areas and among economically weaker sections. Schemes like Pradhan Mantri Jeevan Jyoti Bima Yojana (PMJJBY) and Pradhan Mantri Suraksha Bima Yojana (PMSBY) offer low-cost group coverage through banks and post offices. These programs make insurance affordable and accessible to those who might otherwise remain uninsured.

B. Customized Products

i. Tailor-Made Coverage

Customized products are insurance policies that are specifically designed to meet the unique needs of individuals, families, or businesses. These may involve choosing optional riders, adjusting coverage limits, or developing entirely new policy features. Customization enhances customer satisfaction by ensuring they pay only for the protection they actually need.

ii. Personalization through Riders and Add-ons

Insurance companies offer a range of riders—optional benefits that can be added to a base policy. Examples include:

Critical illness riders

Accidental death benefit riders

Waiver of premium riders

Customers can personalize their plans according to life stage, profession, or risk profile. For instance, a diabetic person may need a health policy with minimal exclusions, or a business traveler may require worldwide coverage with emergency evacuation benefits.

iii. Industry and Occupation-Specific Policies

Businesses, too, often require customized solutions. A logistics company may need fleet insurance with GPS integration, while a software firm may require cyber liability insurance with data breach protection. High-net-worth individuals (HNIs) may prefer customized wealth protection plans, high-value home insurance, or legacy planning tools.

2.5 Consumer Behavior in Insurance Purchase

Understanding consumer behavior in the context of insurance is vital for insurers, agents, and policymakers alike. Unlike other financial products, insurance involves a complex blend of rational planning and emotional decision-making. The product being purchased is not a tangible good but a promise of future financial security, which makes buying behavior in insurance more nuanced. From awareness to final purchase, several internal and external factors affect how and why people choose specific policies.

Consumer behavior in insurance is influenced by personal characteristics like age, income, health status, and education, as well as by social, cultural, and psychological factors. In addition, trust in the insurer, previous experiences with claims, financial literacy, and risk tolerance all play a major role. Insurance decisions are also shaped by behavioral biases, marketing strategies, peer influence, and institutional credibility.

2.5.1 Factors Influencing Buying Decisions

Insurance is not a product that people purchase frequently or impulsively. It is typically bought with careful thought, after evaluating the potential risks and long-term benefits. Unlike tangible goods, insurance represents a future promise of financial security, and as a result, several personal, social, economic, and psychological factors influence a consumer's decision to buy it.

i. Individual's income level:

One of the primary determinants is the individual's income level. People with higher incomes are more likely to buy comprehensive or investment-linked insurance plans, such as ULIPs, retirement savings plans, or whole life insurance. In contrast, individuals from lower-income groups may focus on essential protection such as term insurance, personal accident cover, or low-premium health policies. Affordability plays a significant role, and many customers weigh the cost of premiums against their current expenses and perceived need for coverage.

ii. Age and life stage:

Age and life stage are equally influential. A young, unmarried person might opt for a basic health or motor insurance plan for legal compliance or minimal risk protection. Meanwhile, middle-aged individuals, especially those with dependents, tend to seek more inclusive policies that cover life, family health, education, or mortgage security. Senior citizens, on the other hand, prioritize medical insurance and pension-linked products due to higher health risks and reduced income certainty.

iii. Risk perception and personal experience:

Risk perception and personal experience also shape insurance buying decisions. Individuals who have previously faced medical emergencies, property damage, or the untimely loss of a family member are more likely to recognize the value of insurance. Their personal or observed experiences often act as strong motivators in prompting insurance purchases.

iv. Social influence:

Social influence is another critical factor. Recommendations from friends, family, or colleagues who have purchased or benefited from insurance can significantly sway decision-making. Conversely, negative word-of-mouth—such as a denied claim or bad customer service—can discourage others from buying insurance from a particular provider.

v. Marketing:

Marketing communication and advertising play a strong psychological role. Insurance companies often use emotional storytelling, celebrity endorsements, and real-life case studies to connect with consumers. A well-crafted message that addresses consumer fears—like illness, death, or financial hardship—can increase a product's appeal and urgency.

Lastly, financial literacy and product knowledge are essential. Consumers who understand insurance terms such as premiums, exclusions, riders, or maturity benefits are more confident and likely to choose appropriate policies. Lack of clarity or perceived complexity often delays or prevents the buying decision altogether.

2.5.2 Role of Trust, Awareness, and Literacy

In the insurance industry, trust, awareness, and literacy serve as foundational pillars that directly influence consumer behavior. Insurance, by nature, involves paying today for a future benefit that may or may not occur. As such, the intangible nature of insurance products makes trust in the provider and the system a critical factor in purchase decisions. If consumers do not believe that the insurer will honor the claim or provide value for money, they are unlikely to invest in the product—regardless of its features or affordability.

Trust is built over time and is influenced by brand reputation, customer service quality, claim settlement history, and transparency in communication. New or lesser-known insurance companies may face difficulties in acquiring customers unless they demonstrate reliability and ethical practices. Trust also extends to intermediaries like agents and brokers—consumers tend to purchase from individuals or platforms they consider knowledgeable, honest, and supportive.

Awareness plays an equally important role. Many potential customers in India, especially in rural and semi-urban areas, are unaware of the full range of insurance products available or the specific risks that insurance can mitigate. For instance, a farmer may not be aware that crop insurance exists to protect against climate-related loss, or a gig economy worker may not realize they can access personal accident coverage at low premiums. Awareness can be improved through targeted communication campaigns, community engagement, and educational drives—often supported by regulators like IRDAI or government schemes.

Financial literacy goes a step further than awareness by ensuring that consumers not only know about insurance products but also understand how they work. This includes concepts like premiums, deductibles, exclusions, claim procedures, and benefits. Low insurance literacy often leads to inappropriate policy selection, underinsurance, or disillusionment during claim rejection. People with better financial literacy are more likely to compare plans, ask the right questions, and choose products that align with their needs and affordability.

2.5.3 Behavioral Biases in Risk Perception

Consumer decisions around insurance are not always rational or calculated—they are often influenced by behavioral biases that distort how individuals perceive risk and make choices. Unlike financial products that offer visible returns (like fixed deposits or mutual funds), insurance deals with uncertainty and fear, making it prone to cognitive distortions. Risk perception, the way an individual interprets the likelihood and severity of potential harm, is central to insurance decisions, and this perception is rarely objective.

One common bias is the "optimism bias", where individuals believe that negative events are less likely to happen to them compared to others. For instance, a young adult may avoid buying health insurance under the belief that they are too healthy to fall ill, even when statistics show otherwise. Similarly, people may underestimate the risk of accidents, theft, or even death, especially if they haven't experienced such events personally or in their immediate social circle.

Another significant bias is "availability heuristic", where people assess the likelihood of a risk based on how easily they can recall examples. For example, if someone recently heard about a friend receiving a large payout from a life insurance policy, they may overestimate the importance of buying such a policy. Conversely, if a neighbor had a poor claims experience, it could lead to an irrational aversion to all insurance products.

The status quo bias also affects insurance purchase. Many individuals prefer to stick to their current state of underinsurance or no insurance rather than navigating the complex process of selecting and purchasing a new policy. This inertia is often reinforced by fear of making the wrong decision or a lack of understanding of policy features.

Additionally, framing effects—how information is presented—can significantly influence decisions. A policy described as "saving ₹2 lakh for your family" may be more attractive than one labeled "life insurance with ₹2 lakh sum assured," even though both mean the same.

To address these behavioral biases, insurers must go beyond selling policies—they must also guide, educate, and emotionally connect with customers. Simplified explanations, relatable examples, and trust-building narratives can help overcome irrational fears and distortions in risk perception. Understanding these biases is key to designing effective insurance products, improving customer outreach, and encouraging more rational and informed insurance purchases.

2.5.4 Impact of Pricing, Claims Experience, and Brand Image

In the decision-making process of purchasing insurance, three interrelated factors—pricing, claims experience, and brand image—play a significant role in shaping consumer preferences. These elements influence both the initial purchase decision and the long-term relationship between the insurer and the policyholder. While pricing determines affordability and perceived value, claims experience builds or breaks trust, and brand image reflects the insurer's reputation and market standing.

i. Pricing: The First Filter

For most consumers, premium pricing is the first and most visible component of an insurance product. Many buyers compare plans primarily on the basis of annual premiums, especially when shopping online or through aggregators. While price-sensitive segments tend to choose lower premiums, others may be willing to pay more if the plan offers broader coverage, value-added services, or a reliable claims process.

However, price alone does not always reflect quality. Inexperienced buyers may choose low-cost policies without understanding limitations such as high deductibles, exclusions, or co-pay clauses. Therefore, insurers must strike a balance between competitive pricing and comprehensive coverage while educating consumers about what they are paying for.

ii. Claims Experience: The Moment of Truth

Regardless of how attractively a policy is marketed, the claims process defines the actual value of insurance. A smooth, transparent, and timely claim settlement creates trust and loyalty. On the other hand, delayed or denied claims, cumbersome paperwork, or poor customer service during a claim can lead to dissatisfaction, negative word-of-mouth, and policy lapses.

Insurers who offer digitized, hassle-free claims systems, dedicated helplines, and proactive updates during the claim process tend to retain customers better. Many consumers also check an insurer's claim settlement ratio (CSR) and online reviews before finalizing their purchase.

iii. Brand Image: Perception and Trust

An insurer's brand image greatly influences consumer decisions, especially in a market where products are complex and intangible. A strong brand is associated with reliability, financial strength, ethical practices, and customer-centric services. Consumers are more likely to choose insurers who have a longstanding presence, recognizable branding, and endorsements from influencers, regulatory bodies, or satisfied customers.

Brand image also influences perceived risk: customers feel more secure buying from companies with a positive reputation, even if the price is slightly higher. This is particularly important for life and health insurance, where the buyer is placing long-term trust in the insurer's ability to deliver at a critical time.

2.6 Role of FinTech and Insurtech in Market Expansion

In the rapidly evolving financial services landscape, FinTech (Financial Technology) and Insurtech (Insurance Technology) are driving significant transformation across the insurance value chain. These technologies are not merely digitizing traditional insurance processes; they are redefining the way insurance is designed, distributed, underwritten, and serviced. Their adoption has made insurance more accessible, efficient, personalized, and inclusive—especially in previously underserved markets like rural areas, low-income groups, and tech-savvy youth.

Insurtech startups and FinTech platforms are introducing innovations in customer acquisition, claims processing, risk assessment, and engagement through mobile apps, chatbots, AI tools, and digital wallets. The result is faster service delivery, reduced operational costs, and higher transparency—all of which enhance customer experience and trust. By leveraging data analytics, cloud computing, and artificial intelligence, insurers are now able to offer tailored products, identify new risk pools, and respond in real-time to customer behavior and feedback.

2.6.1 Innovations in Product Design and Personalization

One of the most visible impacts of FinTech and Insurtech in the insurance industry is the transformation of product design. Traditional insurance products were standardized, rigid, and difficult to understand. However, the rise of technology-driven insurance models has led to the development of flexible, user-specific, and modular insurance solutions, addressing diverse customer needs more accurately and affordably.

Personalization in insurance is being driven by data analytics, behavioral profiling, and real-time monitoring tools. FinTech platforms and mobile apps collect customer data—such as lifestyle habits, health indicators, location, or spending patterns—and help insurers offer customized coverage that aligns with individual risk profiles. For example, health insurers now use data from fitness trackers and wearable devices to design wellness-based plans that reward customers for healthy behaviors such as walking 10,000 steps a day or maintaining regular sleep patterns.

In the auto insurance space, usage-based insurance (UBI) has emerged as a game changer. Instead of charging fixed premiums, insurers analyze driving behavior using telematics—monitoring speed, braking habits, travel frequency, and distance—to calculate fair and dynamic premiums. Safe drivers thus pay lower premiums, incentivizing better driving and reducing risk.

Insurtech startups have also introduced bite-sized or sachet insurance products that are short-term and highly specific. These include insurance for one-day train journeys, phone screen damage, dengue hospitalization, or even gig worker protection. Such products are popular among youth, daily wage earners, and low-income groups, who were earlier left out of traditional insurance markets.

Furthermore, the trend of à-la-carte or modular insurance allows policyholders to choose only the components they need—such as maternity, critical illness, or outpatient care—rather than purchasing a comprehensive plan. This flexibility makes insurance more relevant and cost-effective.

The entire buying process is now digital and instant—policies can be customized, quoted, purchased, and stored through mobile apps or digital wallets. Chatbots, robo-advisors, and AI assistants enhance the experience by offering personalized suggestions and real-time assistance.

2.6.2 Use of Big Data, AI, and IoT in Underwriting

Underwriting is the process by which insurers assess the risk of an applicant and decide the terms and pricing of the policy. Traditionally, this process relied heavily on paperwork, manual reviews, and historical data. With the advent of Big Data, Artificial Intelligence (AI), and the Internet of Things (IoT), underwriting has become faster, smarter, and more accurate. Big Data refers to extremely large datasets generated from various sources—social media, mobile apps, wearable devices, transaction records, and online behavior. Insurers use Big Data analytics to gain deep insights into consumer behavior, lifestyle risks, and financial habits. For example, an insurer can analyze a customer's fitness app data, online purchase behavior, and credit score to build a comprehensive risk profile, reducing reliance on just age and income.

Artificial Intelligence enhances the speed and accuracy of decision-making in underwriting. AI algorithms can assess hundreds of variables in seconds, detect fraudulent patterns, and recommend policy terms with precision. Machine learning models improve over time as they learn from claim histories and behavioral trends, making underwriting more adaptive and less biased. AI also powers chatbots and automated advisors that collect data from customers during onboarding, simplifying and speeding up the process.

Internet of Things (IoT) devices such as smart watches, health bands, GPS trackers, and home sensors provide real-time, continuous data about customer activities and conditions. For instance, a smart home device can detect fire, water leakage, or intrusion risks, helping insurers offer dynamic home insurance plans with proactive risk mitigation alerts. In auto insurance, IoT devices track driving behavior to enable real-time pricing and prevent accidents.

These technologies also support predictive underwriting, where insurers estimate the likelihood of claims based on predictive models rather than historical averages. This reduces overcharging and underinsurance, promoting fairness and transparency.

2.6.3 Instant Policy Issuance and Digital KYC

One of the most impactful contributions of FinTech and Insurtech to the insurance industry is the digitization of policy issuance and Know Your Customer (KYC) processes. Traditionally, insurance issuance involved multiple physical documents, in-person verification, and long waiting periods for policy approval. This often led to customer frustration, paperwork errors, and high drop-out rates. With the advent of digital KYC (e-KYC) and real-time policy issuance, insurers have now moved toward a seamless and efficient process that enhances customer experience and operational efficiency.

Digital KYC allows customers to complete their identity verification using Aadhaar-based authentication, PAN verification, or video-based KYC through mobile apps and websites. It eliminates the need for physical visits, photocopies, and manual signatures. This is especially useful in reaching remote and rural customers, as digital KYC can be completed with just a smartphone and internet access. Additionally, video KYC ensures regulatory compliance while enhancing security and fraud prevention.

The use of optical character recognition (OCR), AI-based identity verification, and document scanning tools further reduces onboarding time. Insurtech platforms can now extract information from uploaded documents automatically, verify it in real time, and validate the customer's credentials with official databases. This enables insurers to complete the entire KYC process within minutes.

Once KYC is completed, insurers can offer instant policy issuance through automation. Customers can fill out their forms online, get quotes, make premium payments digitally (via UPI, net banking, or wallets), and receive their policy documents immediately via email or app. This instant issuance capability significantly reduces turnaround time from days to minutes, removing traditional friction points.

Moreover, pre-approved or pre-underwritten policies based on customer profiles allow even faster issuance, especially for low-risk customers who may not require additional medical checks or detailed underwriting.

2.6.4 Collaborations between Startups and Traditional Insurers

The rise of Insurtech startups has not only brought innovation into the insurance ecosystem but has also led to a growing trend of collaboration between startups and traditional insurance companies. While startups bring agility, digital capabilities, and user-centric solutions, traditional insurers bring trust, regulatory experience, and extensive distribution networks. Together, these partnerships are reshaping the insurance landscape and driving market expansion at an accelerated pace.

Startups often focus on solving specific pain points in the insurance value chain—such as digital onboarding, claims automation, chat-based servicing, or AI-powered risk assessment.

However, they may lack the capital reserves, regulatory licenses, or large customer base required to operate independently. On the other hand, large insurance companies may have legacy systems, slower innovation cycles, and limited flexibility in experimenting with new-age technology.

By collaborating, both parties leverage their strengths. For example, Insurtech startups may act as technology enablers, providing digital infrastructure for insurers to launch app-based services, online portals, or API-driven integrations with aggregators. Some startups work as third-party administrators (TPAs) or digital brokers, helping insurers digitize distribution, customer support, and claims processing.

One notable model is the "Insurance-as-a-Service" platform, where a startup offers a cloud-based platform allowing insurers to launch, manage, and scale new products digitally. Another is the embedded insurance model, where insurance is bundled seamlessly with other products—such as ride-hailing apps offering travel insurance, or e-commerce sites offering device protection plans—driven by startup tech and backed by traditional insurers.

Collaborations also include sandbox initiatives approved by regulators like IRDAI in India, where insurers and startups co-develop pilot projects under relaxed compliance norms. This enables innovation without risk to consumers.

These partnerships lead to faster go-to-market times, increased insurance penetration, and accessto newer customer segments such as millennials, gig workers, and first-time policyholders. Traditional insurers gain agility and digital relevance, while startups benefit from scale and credibility.

For Quick Revision

2.1 Insurance Product Segmentation

Insurance products are classified into two major segments—Life Insurance and General Insurance—based on the type of risk they cover.

2.1.1 Life Insurance Products:

- Term Plans: Offer pure life coverage for a fixed term; no maturity benefit; affordable.
- Endowment Plans: Provide both insurance and savings; a lump sum is paid on maturity or death.
- ULIPs (Unit Linked Insurance Plans): Combine insurance with market-linked investment options.

2.1.2 General Insurance Products:

- Health Insurance: Covers hospitalization, surgery, and medical treatment expenses.
- Motor Insurance: Mandatory for vehicles; covers third-party liability and own damage.
- Crop Insurance: Protects farmers from crop failure due to natural calamities or pests.
- Fire and Marine Insurance: Covers loss from fire or damages during the transportation of goods.

2.2 Emerging Insurance Products

- These are modern insurance solutions catering to new and evolving risks.
- Cyber Insurance: Covers losses from cyber threats like hacking or data breaches.
- Travel Insurance: Offers protection against trip cancellations, lost baggage, or medical emergencies abroad.
- Microinsurance: Low-premium policies designed for low-income individuals or rural populations.
- Pandemic and Climate Risk Insurance: Provides coverage against losses from pandemics or extreme weather events.

2.3 Distribution Channels in Insurance

- Multiple channels are used to reach different customer segments effectively.

2.3.1 Agency System

- Individual Agents: Sell policies on commission; serve as personal advisors.

- Corporate Agents: Institutions selling insurance alongside their core offerings (e.g., NBFCs, banks).
- Training and Licensing: Mandatory training and exams ensure agents are certified.

2.3.2 Bancassurance

- Involves partnerships between banks and insurance companies.
- Models: Referral, corporate agency, or joint venture.
- Revenue is shared between the bank and the insurer.

2.3.3 Digital and Online Platforms

- Aggregators: Websites like Policy Bazaar that compare policies.
- D2C Sales: Direct purchases via insurer websites or apps.

2.4 Customer Segmentation and Targeting

- Insurers classify customers into segments for targeted marketing and product development.

2.4.1 Urban vs. Rural Markets

- Urban customers seek investment-linked and customized products.
- Rural markets need low-cost, basic coverage options.

2.4.2 MSMEs and Corporates

- Require policies like group health, asset, liability, and business interruption insurance.

2.4.3 Gender-Based and Age-Based Segmentation

- Women, senior citizens, and millennials have different risk profiles and insurance needs.

2.4.4 Group Insurance and Customized Products

- Group insurance offers uniform coverage to employees or members.
- Customized policies meet specific needs (e.g., cancer care, maternity coverage).

2.5 Consumer Behavior in Insurance Purchase

- Understanding how consumers decide helps in better product design and marketing.

2.5.1 Factors Influencing Buying Decisions

- Income, family needs, financial goals, and past experiences shape decisions.

2.5.2 Role of Trust, Awareness, and Literacy

- Low awareness and mistrust in insurers can reduce policy adoption.

2.5.3 Behavioral Biases in Risk Perception

- People may underestimate or overestimate risks due to emotions or misinformation.

2.5.4 Pricing, Claims Experience, and Brand Image

- Fair pricing, quick claims settlement, and strong brand influence customer loyalty.

2.6 Role of FinTech and Insurtech in Market Expansion

- Technological innovation is reshaping the insurance sector.

2.6.1 Innovations in Product Design and Personalization

- Tailor-made plans based on age, health, or lifestyle preferences.

2.6.2 Use of Big Data, AI, and IoT in Underwriting

- Predictive models assess risk better; wearable devices provide real-time health data.

2.6.3 Instant Policy Issuance and Digital KYC

- Speeds up onboarding; reduces paperwork; improves user convenience.

2.6.4 Collaborations between Startups and Traditional Insurers

- Brings together agility and trust; leads to better product innovation and outreach.

Test Your Knowledge

2-Marks Questions

1. Define Term Insurance with an example.
2. Mention any two features of Endowment Plans.
3. What is a Unit Linked Insurance Plan (ULIP)?
4. List any two types of General Insurance products.
5. What do you mean by Cyber Insurance?
6. State any two features of Travel Insurance.
7. Who are the target beneficiaries of Microinsurance?
8. What is Pandemic Risk Insurance?
9. Name any two functions of an Individual Insurance Agent.
10. What is Bancassurance?
11. Give any two benefits of digital insurance platforms.
12. What is the role of aggregators like Policy Bazaar in insurance?
13. State any two differences between urban and rural insurance markets.
14. Define group insurance with one example.
15. Mention any two factors that influence insurance purchase decisions.
16. What is meant by "insurance literacy"?
17. How does brand image affect consumer decisions in insurance?
18. Give any two examples of behavioral biases in insurance purchase.
19. What is personalized insurance in the context of InsurTech?
20. Define digital KYC in insurance onboarding.
21. Mention two applications of Big Data in underwriting.
22. What is the importance of mobile apps in insurance sales?
23. Write any two advantages of chatbots in policy servicing.
24. Name any two collaborative models between startups and insurers.
25. State any two insurance needs of MSMEs.

5-Marks Questions

1. Differentiate between various Life Insurance products with suitable examples.
2. Analyze the scope and features of General Insurance products in India.

3. Explain the relevance and structure of emerging insurance products like Cyber and Climate Risk Insurance.
4. Evaluate the effectiveness of Microinsurance in addressing the needs of low-income groups.
5. Compare and contrast individual agents, corporate agents, and digital platforms as distribution channels.
6. Discuss the functioning of Bancassurance with models and revenue-sharing mechanisms.
7. Assess the impact of digitalization and mobile technology on insurance distribution.
8. Examine the role of chatbots and AI in enhancing customer engagement in the insurance sector.
9. Analyze the insurance needs of rural vs. urban markets and suggest ways to bridge the gap.
10. Discuss how insurance companies segment customers based on gender, age, and income.
11. Explain the concept of customized group insurance with examples of corporates or institutions.
12. Identify and evaluate key factors that influence consumer behavior in insurance purchase.
13. How do pricing, brand image, and past claims experiences affect a customer's insurance decision?
14. Explain behavioral biases in risk perception and how insurers can address them.
15. Discuss the contribution of FinTech and InsurTech in expanding insurance reach and efficiency.
16. Evaluate how Big Data and AI are revolutionizing underwriting processes in the insurance industry.
17. Describe the innovations in product design and personalization enabled by technology.
18. Explain the process and benefits of instant policy issuance through digital KYC.
19. Examine how collaborations between traditional insurers and startups are reshaping the insurance ecosystem.
20. Propose a new digital insurance product for a niche segment (e.g., gig workers, urban women, elderly) and justify its need and features.

Chapter 3

Trends, Challenges, and Opportunities in Insurance Market

3.1 Growth Drivers of the Indian Insurance Sector

The Indian insurance sector has witnessed significant growth due to multiple interrelated drivers. A major factor is the increase in financial literacy and awareness, which has led more individuals to understand the importance of risk protection and long-term financial planning. Additionally, the government's push for financial inclusion through schemes like PMJDY, PMSBY, and PMJJBY has brought insurance access to underserved populations, especially in rural areas. The expanding middle class and rapid urbanization have also contributed, as rising incomes and lifestyle changes have increased the demand for life, health, and general insurance. Furthermore, tax benefits under Sections 80C and 10(10D) act as financial incentives for people to invest in insurance products. Together, these factors have widened the customer base, encouraged product innovation, and improved policy penetration across urban and rural India, making these growth drivers essential for the sustainable development of the Indian insurance industry.

3.1.1 Increasing Financial Literacy and Awareness

Financial literacy plays a crucial role in the expansion of the insurance sector. It refers to individuals' ability to understand financial concepts and use them effectively to manage personal finances. In India, low financial literacy has traditionally been a barrier to insurance adoption. However, with growing efforts from the government, IRDAI, banks, insurers, and NGOs, there has been a noticeable improvement in people's understanding of insurance. Programs like the National Strategy for Financial Education by the RBI and Insurance Awareness Campaigns by IRDAI have educated citizens on the importance of risk protection and the benefits of being insured. These initiatives are often targeted at school children, college students, women, rural populations, and small business owners. As a result, more individuals are now aware of the need for insurance, how to compare products, and the procedures for policy claims and renewals.

The digital revolution has also enhanced financial awareness. Mobile apps, online portals, and social media have become powerful tools for learning about insurance. Consumers can now access policy details, calculate premiums, and read reviews before buying policies, leading to more informed decision-making.

Increased awareness has changed the perception of insurance from being a mere tax-saving tool to a financial necessity. People are beginning to see insurance as a safety net against unforeseen events such as accidents, illnesses, and death. This shift in mindset has led to higher demand for life, health, and general insurance products, making financial literacy a key growth driver in the Indian insurance market.

3.1.2 Government Push for Financial Inclusion

The Indian government's strong focus on financial inclusion has significantly contributed to the growth of the insurance sector. Financial inclusion refers to the process of ensuring access to financial services, including insurance, to all segments of the society—especially the underprivileged and low-income groups. Recognizing that a vast portion of India's population lacked access to formal financial services, the government launched a series of ambitious initiatives to bring them into the financial mainstream.

Schemes like Pradhan Mantri Jan Dhan Yojana (PMJDY) have been instrumental in this effort. PMJDY facilitated the opening of millions of bank accounts for previously unbanked individuals. With banking access established, these individuals became eligible for various government-backed insurance schemes such as Pradhan Mantri Suraksha Bima Yojana (PMSBY) for accident insurance and Pradhan Mantri Jeevan Jyoti Bima Yojana (PMJJBY) for life insurance. These low-cost schemes have enabled millions to secure insurance coverage for the first time.

The government has also encouraged insurers to expand their reach in rural and semi-urban areas by relaxing regulations and promoting the use of digital platforms. Public Sector insurers are mandated to operate in remote areas, while private insurers are incentivized to offer microinsurance and health policies targeting economically weaker sections.

Digital initiatives such as the Jan Suraksha Abhiyan, e-insurance accounts, and the integration of insurance services with Aadhaar have streamlined policy issuance and claim processes, making insurance more accessible and user-friendly.

Through financial inclusion, the government has succeeded in creating a broader customer base for insurance companies. This push has not only increased the number of policyholders but has also driven product innovation and competitive pricing, thereby contributing to the robust growth of the Indian insurance sector.

3.1.3 Rising Middle Class and Urbanization

India's rising middle class and rapid urbanization have emerged as strong growth drivers for the insurance industry. The middle class, characterized by stable incomes, increasing disposable earnings, and aspirations for a better quality of life, represents a key target market for insurers. As income levels rise, individuals and families are more likely to seek financial products that offer protection, long-term savings, and security—needs that insurance products are well-positioned to fulfill.

Urbanization has brought about lifestyle changes, increased health risks, and greater financial responsibilities. Urban consumers are more exposed to market risks, road accidents, medical expenses, and property damages. Consequently, there is a growing need for health insurance, vehicle insurance, home insurance, and life insurance among urban residents. Moreover, the demand for retirement planning, child education plans, and investment-linked insurance products is on the rise in urban middle-class households.

With urbanization also comes better access to technology and digital infrastructure. Middle-class consumers, especially the younger population in Tier I and Tier II cities, prefer purchasing insurance online, comparing policies, and using mobile apps for policy servicing. This tech-savvy behavior has enabled insurers to launch innovative, paperless, and instant insurance solutions that appeal to this demographic.

In addition, lifestyle aspirations among the urban middle class have led to increased awareness about the importance of future planning. Events such as the COVID-19 pandemic have further heightened the perception of vulnerability, prompting many to invest in health and life insurance as a financial safeguard.

Therefore, the growing size of India's middle class, combined with ongoing urbanization and increasing digital access, is expanding the customer base and fueling the growth of the insurance sector significantly.

3.1.4 Tax Benefits under Sections 80C and 10(10D)

The Indian Income Tax Act provides attractive tax incentives that promote insurance purchases, making tax benefits a key growth driver of the insurance industry. Under Section 80C, individuals can claim a deduction of up to ₹1.5 lakh on premiums paid for life insurance policies. This benefit is available for policies covering self, spouse, or children, encouraging salaried and self-employed individuals to consider life insurance not only for protection but also as a tax-saving tool.

Additionally, under Section 10(10D), the maturity proceeds of a life insurance policy are exempt from income tax, provided certain conditions are met (such as the premium not exceeding 10% of the sum assured for policies issued after April 1, 2012). This tax-free return feature makes life insurance policies, especially traditional endowment and ULIP plans, an attractive investment option for long-term savings and wealth accumulation.

Health insurance also offers tax advantages under Section 80D, which allows deductions on premiums paid for health insurance policies for self, spouse, children, and parents. This provision has contributed to the growing popularity of health insurance products among the urban population.

These tax benefits act as a dual incentive—providing financial protection while reducing the overall tax liability. Many individuals choose to purchase insurance primarily during the tax-planning season, which leads to a seasonal surge in policy sales.

Insurers have capitalized on these provisions by designing products tailored to meet both protection and tax-saving objectives. Marketing campaigns highlighting the tax advantages of insurance products also play a key role in influencing buying decisions.

3.2 Emerging Market Trends

The digital transformation of the Indian insurance industry marks a paradigm shift in how insurance products are marketed, sold, and serviced. Traditionally, insurance was largely dependent on in-person agent interactions, paper-based documentation, and lengthy approval processes. However, the integration of digital technologies has revolutionized these practices, making insurance more accessible, efficient, and customer-centric.

One of the most significant changes is the availability of online platforms for policy servicing. Customers can now compare different insurance products, calculate premiums, make purchases, renew policies, and even file claims online—without visiting a physical office. This transformation has been fueled by the increasing internet and smartphone penetration across the country. Insurance companies have developed mobile applications and responsive websites that offer 24/7 service, thereby enhancing customer convenience and satisfaction.

Digital tools such as chatbots, automated underwriting, AI-driven claim processing, and e-KYC (Know Your Customer) have further streamlined the customer experience. Policy issuance, which earlier took days or even weeks, can now be completed in minutes through digital verification and payment systems. Moreover, document management has shifted to cloud-based systems, allowing for easy access and retrieval of policies and claim forms.

Another key area of digital advancement is the use of data analytics and machine learning to analyze customer behavior, assess risks, and design customized products. This not only improves operational efficiency but also helps in fraud detection and enhances regulatory compliance.

Digital transformation is also driving financial inclusion, as insurance companies can now reach remote areas through online campaigns, video consultations, and vernacular content. Insurtech startups are playing a pivotal role by introducing innovative digital solutions that challenge conventional models.

3.2.1 Digital Transformation and Online Policy Servicing

The digital transformation of the Indian insurance industry marks a paradigm shift in how insurance products are marketed, sold, and serviced. Traditionally, insurance was largely dependent on in-person agent interactions, paper-based documentation, and lengthy approval processes. However, the integration of digital technologies has revolutionized these practices, making insurance more accessible, efficient, and customer-centric.

One of the most significant changes is the availability of online platforms for policy servicing. Customers can now compare different insurance products, calculate premiums, make purchases, renew policies, and even file claims online—without visiting a physical office. This transformation has been fueled by the increasing internet and smartphone penetration across the country. Insurance companies have developed mobile applications and responsive websites that offer 24/7 service, thereby enhancing customer convenience and satisfaction.

Digital tools such as chatbots, automated underwriting, AI-driven claim processing, and e-KYC (Know Your Customer) have further streamlined the customer experience. Policy issuance, which earlier took days or even weeks, can now be completed in minutes through digital verification and payment systems. Moreover, document management has shifted to cloud-based systems, allowing for easy access and retrieval of policies and claim forms.

Another key area of digital advancement is the use of data analytics and machine learning to analyze customer behavior, assess risks, and design customized products. This not only improves operational efficiency but also helps in fraud detection and enhances regulatory compliance.

Digital transformation is also driving financial inclusion, as insurance companies can now reach remote areas through online campaigns, video consultations, and vernacular content. Insurtech startups are playing a pivotal role by introducing innovative digital solutions that challenge conventional models.

3.2.2 Demand for Personalized and Need-Based Policies

In recent years, there has been a growing demand for personalized and need-based insurance policies in India. Consumers today are more informed, aware, and financially conscious than ever before. With increased access to online information and comparison tools, they expect insurance solutions that are tailored to their specific needs, life goals, and risk profiles—rather than generic, one-size-fits-all products.

Traditional insurance policies often lacked flexibility, offering standardized benefits and fixed terms. However, modern customers—especially millennials and Gen Z—seek policies that align with their lifestyles, occupations, health status, and family responsibilities. For example, a young working professional may prefer a policy with lower premiums and high accidental coverage, while a middle-aged individual might prioritize critical illness or long-term savings plans.

To cater to these expectations, insurers are increasingly adopting data-driven personalization strategies. With the help of advanced analytics, artificial intelligence (AI), and customer profiling, companies can recommend policies that match a customer's financial goals, health data, and life stage. This trend has given rise to flexible plans that allow policyholders to choose their own sum assured, policy tenure, premium payment frequency, riders, and even investment strategies in the case of ULIPs (Unit Linked Insurance Plans).

Moreover, insurers are now offering modular insurance products, where customers can select only the components they require. For example, health insurance buyers can opt for maternity benefits, outpatient treatment, or mental health coverage as add-ons.

This shift towards need-based policies also supports customer retention and trust. A policyholder who feels their specific concerns are addressed is more likely to remain loyal and recommend the insurer to others.

3.2.3 Usage-Based and On-Demand Insurance Products

Another emerging trend in the Indian insurance market is the development and growing popularity of usage-based and on-demand insurance products. These models break away from the traditional annual, fixed-coverage format and instead provide flexibility, affordability, and relevance by allowing consumers to pay premiums based on actual usage or short-term needs.

Usage-based insurance (UBI) is especially prominent in the motor insurance segment. Enabled by telematics technology, UBI policies track driver behavior, mileage, speed, and location to calculate premiums more accurately. Customers who drive less or drive more safely can benefit from lower premiums. This system not only incentivizes responsible driving but also appeals to urban users who own vehicles but do not drive them frequently.

On-demand insurance, on the other hand, allows users to activate or deactivate coverage for specific durations or purposes. For example, a traveler can purchase travel insurance only for the days of the trip, or a student studying abroad can buy coverage for just a semester. Similarly, gig economy workers, freelancers, and delivery personnel can buy insurance for work-related risks during their job hours only.

The rise of digital platforms and mobile apps has made such flexible products easier to implement and manage. Customers can now turn coverage on and off with a few taps on their smartphones, giving them control and transparency over their insurance.

These products also suit millennials and Gen Z, who value flexibility and are less likely to commit to long-term contracts. Moreover, they meet the needs of a rapidly changing workforce and lifestyle trends, including shared mobility, short-term rentals, and freelance work.

By offering tailored, pay-as-you-go solutions, usage-based and on-demand insurance products improve affordability and accessibility, especially for low-income or first-time buyers. They are expected to play a vital role in expanding insurance penetration in India's diverse and evolving market.

3.2.4 Growth in Term and Health Insurance Post-Pandemic

The COVID-19 pandemic significantly changed consumer behavior and priorities, especially regarding health and financial security. As a result, there has been a noticeable surge in demand for term insurance and health insurance products across India. The pandemic served as a wake-up call, making individuals and families realize the importance of protection-oriented insurance coverage.

Term insurance, known for its affordability and high coverage, witnessed increased adoption as people became more aware of the need for income protection in case of an untimely death. Many first-time buyers entered the insurance market seeking policies that would safeguard their family's future, especially in uncertain economic conditions. Insurance companies responded by launching simplified, digitally accessible term plans with flexible payment options, riders like critical illness cover, and accelerated claim settlement.

Simultaneously, the importance of health insurance became more prominent than ever before. The high cost of COVID-19 treatment and hospitalization highlighted the inadequacy of relying solely on employer-provided coverage or savings. This prompted many individuals to buy comprehensive health plans, upgrade their existing policies, or add coverage for critical illness and post-hospitalization care.

The pandemic also encouraged the purchase of family floater plans, senior citizen health insurance, and top-up covers. There was a surge in demand for cashless claim facilities, home treatment benefits, and digital consultation services, which insurers have increasingly incorporated.

Regulatory support from IRDAI, including faster claim processing and the introduction of standardized products like Arogya Sanjeevani, helped boost consumer trust and ease of access.

3.3 Challenges in the Insurance Industry

The Indian insurance industry faces several critical challenges that hinder its growth and effectiveness. A major issue is low insurance penetration and limited awareness, particularly in rural and semi-urban areas, where people often lack knowledge about insurance benefits. This is compounded by delays in claim settlement, which erode customer trust due to complex procedures and slow processing times. Another significant challenge is mis-selling of insurance products and the lack of transparency in policy terms, which leads to customer dissatisfaction and early policy lapses. Additionally, the industry struggles with a complex regulatory and compliance burden, requiring constant adaptation to evolving IRDAI guidelines, which can strain smaller companies and InsurTech firms. These challenges collectively affect customer confidence, market expansion, and operational efficiency. To ensure sustainable growth, the sector must focus on improving awareness, streamlining claims, ensuring ethical sales practices, and balancing regulation with ease of doing business.

3.3.1 Low Insurance Penetration and Awareness Gaps

One of the most persistent challenges facing the Indian insurance industry is the low level of insurance penetration, which refers to the ratio of total insurance premiums to the Gross Domestic Product (GDP). Despite being one of the fastest-growing economies in the world, India's insurance penetration remains below the global average. This indicates that a large segment of the population either does not have insurance or is underinsured.

Several factors contribute to this issue. First and foremost is the lack of awareness about the importance of insurance as a tool for risk management and financial protection. In many rural and semi-urban areas, people still view insurance as an unnecessary expense or a product meant only for the wealthy. Many individuals associate insurance only with tax savings or consider it relevant only in the case of death, without understanding the broader benefits related to health, property, or income protection.

Another challenge is limited access to insurance infrastructure. In remote regions, the absence of insurance agents, digital connectivity issues, and poor financial literacy further widen the protection gap. Even in urban areas, consumers often lack clarity on policy features, exclusions, and claim procedures, which deters them from purchasing insurance.

Moreover, complex jargon, inadequate promotion of government schemes, and insufficient digital literacy limit participation among potential first-time policyholders. Efforts by IRDAI, insurers, and NGOs have helped improve awareness, but progress remains uneven across states and income groups.

Tackling this challenge requires a multi-pronged approach involving awareness campaigns in regional languages, school-level financial education, and simplifying insurance products. Increasing the availability of microinsurance and bundling insurance with essential services (like loans or health check-ups) can also help bridge the gap. Unless insurance awareness and accessibility are improved, the Indian insurance market will remain far below its true potential.

3.3.2 Delays in Claim Settlement and Trust Deficit

Timely and hassle-free claim settlement is one of the most important aspects of customer satisfaction in the insurance industry. However, delays in claim processing remain a significant concern in India and are a major contributor to the trust deficit between insurers and policyholders. Customers often cite delayed payments, complicated documentation requirements, and lack of transparency in the claim process as reasons for dissatisfaction.

In many cases, especially in life and health insurance, claimants face long waiting periods due to manual verification processes, inadequate coordination between service providers, and incomplete or unclear policy documentation. Sometimes, policyholders are unaware of the conditions required for claim approval, which leads to claim rejections and a perception of unfair treatment. This weakens consumer confidence and discourages others from buying insurance.

Furthermore, low levels of insurance literacy aggravate the issue. Policyholders often misunderstand the terms and exclusions in the contract, and in the absence of proper agent guidance, they may submit inaccurate or insufficient claim documents. This can delay or deny rightful settlements. In rural areas, the situation is worse due to poor access to claim assistance services and limited digital infrastructure.

The issue is not only limited to private insurers; even public sector companies with high claim loads often struggle with efficiency. While the IRDAI mandates timelines for claim processing and has introduced grievance redressal mechanisms, enforcement and customer awareness remain limited.

To address this, insurers are now adopting digital claim processing systems, AI-based fraud detection, and simplified online claim intimation tools. However, building trust will require consistent communication, better customer support, and increased transparency. Establishing fast-track claim settlement procedures, especially for smaller amounts or emergency claims, can also help restore confidence. Resolving this challenge is essential for building a robust and trustworthy insurance ecosystem in India.

3.3.3 Mis-selling and Lack of Transparency

Mis-selling of insurance products is a widespread issue in the Indian insurance industry and one that undermines consumer confidence and long-term growth. Mis-selling occurs when customers are sold products that do not match their needs or when they are given incomplete or misleading information about the policy's features, returns, or exclusions. This unethical practice often results in dissatisfaction, policy lapses, and legal disputes.

Insurance is a complex product, and many buyers—especially first-time or less-educated customers—depend heavily on agents or intermediaries for guidance. Unfortunately, some agents prioritize commission over customer interest and push high-premium products without adequately explaining the terms and conditions. In some cases, customers are not informed about the policy's lock-in period, limited benefits, or non-guaranteed returns, leading to unrealistic expectations.

Additionally, lack of transparency in policy documents makes it difficult for buyers to fully understand what they are purchasing. Long and complicated contracts, legal jargon, and hidden charges can confuse policyholders. Even digitally literate consumers find it challenging to compare policies or assess whether the product meets their needs. Mis-selling is particularly common in life insurance and investment-linked products, where the line between protection and savings is blurred.

The consequences of mis-selling are severe. It leads to early policy surrenders, loss of customer trust, negative public perception, and reputational damage for insurers. It also increases regulatory scrutiny and legal liability for the companies involved.

Regulatory bodies like IRDAI have taken steps to curb this problem by issuing guidelines on agent training, product disclosures, and suitability norms. The introduction of standardized products like Saral Jeevan Bima and Arogya Sanjeevani is aimed at improving transparency and comparability.

To effectively tackle mis-selling, the industry must invest in ethical sales training, improve digital literacy among customers, and promote transparent communication. A shift from commission-driven sales to need-based advisory will be key to ensuring long-term trust and sustainability.

3.3.4 Complex Regulatory and Compliance Burden

The Indian insurance industry operates under a detailed and highly regulated framework designed to ensure consumer protection, financial stability, and market discipline. While regulation is essential, the complex and evolving nature of compliance requirements presents a significant challenge for insurers, especially newer players and small-scale insurance companies.

The Insurance Regulatory and Development Authority of India (IRDAI) issues guidelines covering almost every aspect of operations—product design, pricing, disclosures, solvency requirements, agent licensing, grievance redressal, and investment norms. While these regulations aim to maintain sectoral integrity and protect policyholders, they often involve multiple layers of documentation, approval cycles, and periodic reporting that increase the operational workload and compliance costs for insurers.

Frequent regulatory updates also require companies to remain agile and continuously adapt their systems and processes. For instance, changes in commission structures, standardization of products, or reporting requirements on ESG (Environmental, Social, and Governance) factors may involve complex IT and human resource adjustments. This is particularly burdensome for smaller insurers and InsurTech startups, who often lack the resources or legal infrastructure to respond quickly to such changes.

In addition, different types of insurance (life, health, general) often face distinct regulatory regimes, creating complexity for companies offering bundled or hybrid products. Cross-border insurance, reinsurance arrangements, and product innovation may also require multiple layers of clearance, slowing down the time-to-market.

Although IRDAI has introduced digital platforms for regulatory filings and promotes a risk-based supervisory approach, insurers still report delays in approval processes and ambiguity in interpreting certain norms.

To overcome these challenges, insurers are increasingly investing in RegTech (regulatory technology) solutions that automate compliance tracking and reporting. There is also a growing demand for simplification and harmonization of regulations to foster innovation and competitiveness.

Balancing robust regulation with operational ease will be essential to support innovation, reduce compliance costs, and ensure the sustained growth of the insurance sector.

3.4 Future Opportunities and Innovation Areas

The Indian insurance industry is poised for rapid innovation and expansion, driven by emerging technologies and evolving customer needs. One major opportunity lies in the integration of HealthTech, enabling insurers to offer preventive care and personalized health services using wearables, telemedicine, and health apps. Another promising area is embedded insurance, where coverage is seamlessly bundled with products or services—such as smartphones, travel bookings, or e-commerce purchases—making insurance more accessible and convenient. Artificial Intelligence (AI) and predictive analytics are revolutionizing underwriting by enabling real-time risk assessment, automated decision-making, and dynamic pricing based on customer behavior. Additionally, the expansion into Tier II and III cities and rural regions opens new markets for microinsurance, health, and crop-related policies. By adopting localized, tech-enabled, and affordable solutions, insurers can reach underserved populations. Collectively, these innovations present vast opportunities to deepen insurance penetration and build a more inclusive, data-driven insurance ecosystem.

3.4.1 HealthTech and Digital Health Integration

The integration of HealthTech with insurance presents a significant future opportunity for innovation and market expansion. HealthTech refers to the use of technology such as wearable devices, telemedicine, electronic health records, and mobile health apps to improve healthcare delivery. For insurers, this integration enables proactive risk management by allowing real-time health monitoring and personalized wellness programs. For instance, wearable fitness trackers can provide insurers with data on the customer's physical activity, sleep patterns, and heart rate, which can be used to offer dynamic premium pricing and rewards for healthy behavior.

Digital health tools also simplify claims processing through digital prescriptions and online consultation records, reducing paperwork and fraud. Telemedicine has emerged as a major value addition, especially in post-pandemic times, by enabling policyholders to consult doctors remotely, which insurers can cover under outpatient benefits.

Insurers are also partnering with HealthTech startups to design preventive health insurance models, focusing on lifestyle management rather than just covering hospitalization. This shift from reactive to preventive care benefits both customers and insurers by reducing claim ratios and promoting better health outcomes. Overall, HealthTech integration is set to redefine how health insurance is delivered and managed, making it more efficient, data-driven, and customer-centric.

3.4.2 Embedded Insurance (Bundled with Products/Services)

Embedded insurance refers to the seamless integration of insurance coverage into the purchase of products or services, often at the point of sale. This innovation makes insurance more accessible and frictionless, especially for first-time or low-ticket buyers. Examples include insurance bundled with smartphones, appliances, airline tickets, cab rides, and even e-commerce deliveries. When a customer buys a product or service, they receive insurance coverage automatically or at a discounted rate, without needing to go through a separate purchase process.

This model offers immense future potential in India, particularly in sectors like consumer electronics, travel, mobility, and agriculture. Embedded insurance is especially attractive to younger, digitally savvy consumers who prefer convenience and quick access to coverage. It also benefits service providers and retailers by adding value to their offerings and enhancing customer satisfaction.

Insurers, on the other hand, benefit from low-cost distribution, access to vast customer data, and improved market penetration. Partnerships between insurers and e-commerce platforms, fintech companies, and OEMs (original equipment manufacturers) are growing rapidly. Embedded insurance helps in closing the protection gap by making insurance an invisible, yet integral part of everyday transactions. Going forward, this approach can revolutionize how insurance is distributed, transforming it from a standalone product into an embedded experience.

3.4.3 Artificial Intelligence and Predictive Analytics in Underwriting

The use of Artificial Intelligence (AI) and predictive analytics is transforming underwriting in the insurance industry, making it faster, more accurate, and customer-centric. Traditionally, underwriting relied on manual processes and static data such as age, income, and past medical history. With AI, insurers can now analyze vast amounts of real-time and behavioral data, including lifestyle habits, transaction history, and digital footprints, to assess risk more precisely.

AI algorithms can automate the underwriting process by analyzing data points in seconds, reducing the turnaround time for policy issuance from days to minutes. Predictive analytics enables insurers to forecast future claims based on patterns and trends, allowing for more customized pricing models. For example, a health insurer can predict the likelihood of chronic illness development and price the premium accordingly or suggest preventive care services. This innovation not only enhances operational efficiency but also reduces fraudulent claims, minimizes underwriting errors, and improves customer experience. It enables the creation of dynamic underwriting models, which adjust risk scores and premiums over time based on updated data inputs.

As AI and analytics tools become more advanced, they will play an increasingly central role in product design, risk management, and customer segmentation, offering a competitive edge to forward-thinking insurers.

3.4.4 Expansion into Tier II and III Cities and Rural Areas

The expansion into Tier II, Tier III cities and rural areas represents a major growth opportunity for the Indian insurance sector. These regions house a significant portion of the population, many of whom remain uninsured or underinsured. With increasing financial literacy, mobile penetration, and economic development in smaller towns and villages, the demand for affordable and relevant insurance products is steadily rising.

These areas present a largely untapped market for microinsurance, health insurance, crop insurance, and livestock protection plans. To serve this segment effectively, insurers must tailor their offerings to local needs, simplify policy language, and reduce documentation requirements. Distribution strategies also need to be localized, leveraging trusted community channels such as cooperative societies, self-help groups, and local banks.

Technology plays a key role in this expansion. Mobile-based platforms, vernacular apps, and assisted digital models can overcome the challenges of reach and literacy. Government initiatives like Digital India and insurance schemes such as PMFBY (Pradhan Mantri Fasal Bima Yojana) and PMJJBY have already laid the foundation for deeper insurance penetration.

The long-term success of insurers will depend on how well they can tap into rural and semi-urban markets with inclusive, simple, and value-driven insurance solutions that meet the unique needs of these communities.

3.5 Government Schemes and Their Market Impact

Government schemes have significantly boosted insurance penetration in India. PMJJBY offers low-cost life insurance to underserved populations, while PMFBY protects farmers against crop losses. Ayushman Bharat (PM-JAY) provides health insurance to over 50 crore citizens, improving access to quality healthcare. These initiatives have introduced millions to formal insurance for the first time. Public-private partnerships in implementing these schemes have enhanced efficiency, scalability, and innovation. Overall, these government programs have expanded the insurance market, improved financial security for vulnerable groups, and supported the goal of inclusive growth in India's evolving insurance landscape.

3.5.1 Pradhan Mantri Jeevan Jyoti Bima Yojana (PMJJBY)

The Pradhan Mantri Jeevan Jyoti Bima Yojana (PMJJBY) is a government-backed life insurance scheme launched in 2015 to promote financial inclusion and provide affordable life cover to low-income groups. The scheme is open to individuals aged 18 to 50 years who hold a savings bank account and consent to auto-debit. For an annual premium of ₹436, it offers a life insurance cover of ₹2 lakh in case of the policyholder's death due to any reason.

PMJJBY has significantly impacted the Indian insurance market by increasing the number of first-time policyholders, especially from rural and underserved segments. The scheme is administered by Life Insurance Corporation (LIC) and other participating life insurers through public and private banks. It operates on a simple enrollment model with automatic annual renewal, making it easy for citizens to access coverage.

The success of PMJJBY lies in its affordability, simplicity, and wide reach. It has increased awareness about life insurance and encouraged more people to see it as a basic financial necessity. From an industry perspective, it has expanded the customer base and opened new channels of distribution, contributing to deeper insurance penetration and supporting the national agenda of inclusive financial protection.

3.5.2 Pradhan Mantri Fasal Bima Yojana (PMFBY)

Launched in 2016, the Pradhan Mantri Fasal Bima Yojana (PMFBY) aims to provide comprehensive crop insurance coverage to farmers against losses due to natural calamities, pests, and diseases. It is one of the largest agricultural insurance schemes in the world and plays a crucial role in safeguarding farmers' incomes and ensuring agricultural stability. The scheme is open to all farmers, with low premium rates—2% for Kharif crops, 1.5% for Rabi crops, and 5% for commercial and horticultural crops. The remaining premium is subsidized by the central and state governments.

PMFBY has had a transformative impact on the insurance market by integrating the agriculture sector into the formal risk management system. It involves collaboration between insurance companies, government agencies, banks, and local authorities. The use of technology such as remote sensing, GPS, and mobile apps for crop loss assessment and claim processing has made the scheme more efficient and transparent.

From a market perspective, PMFBY has opened up opportunities for agri-insurance product innovation, increased rural outreach, and created demand for better risk assessment tools. It also supports insurers in building specialized capabilities for rural markets. Despite implementation challenges, the scheme remains central to India's goal of improving farmers' resilience and expanding insurance access in the agricultural sector.

3.5.3 Ayushman Bharat and Health Insurance Expansion

Ayushman Bharat – Pradhan Mantri Jan Arogya Yojana (PM-JAY), launched in 2018, is one of the world's largest government-funded health insurance schemes. It aims to provide financial protection to over 50 crore people, primarily from low-income and vulnerable groups. The scheme offers a coverage of ₹5 lakh per family per year for secondary and tertiary hospitalization, across a wide network of empaneled public and private hospitals.

Ayushman Bharat has significantly influenced the health insurance landscape in India by bringing millions of previously uninsured individuals into the formal healthcare system. The scheme encourages preventive care, early treatment, and access to quality medical services without financial hardship. Its implementation through a digital platform ensures paperless, cashless transactions and efficient claims management.

The market impact of Ayushman Bharat is substantial. It has spurred infrastructure development in Tier II and Tier III cities, increased demand for health-related services, and incentivized insurers and healthcare providers to innovate and scale operations. It also fosters public-private collaboration and creates opportunities for insurance product bundling, telemedicine, and digital health integration.

By expanding the healthcare safety net, Ayushman Bharat contributes to long-term health financing reforms and plays a key role in increasing health insurance penetration in India's underserved regions.

3.5.4 Role of Public-Private Partnerships in Insurance Access

Public-Private Partnerships (PPPs) play a crucial role in improving insurance access and efficiency in India, particularly in reaching underserved and vulnerable populations. These partnerships combine the regulatory oversight, funding, and reach of government institutions with the technological innovation, distribution networks, and customer service capabilities of private sector insurers. PPPs have been instrumental in implementing large-scale schemes such as PMJJBY, PMSBY, Ayushman Bharat, and PMFBY.

Through PPPs, insurers can deliver standardized and affordable products while leveraging government support for subsidies, outreach, and infrastructure. Governments, in turn, benefit from the efficiency, scalability, and innovation that private players bring. For instance, under PMFBY, private insurers work with state governments to assess crop losses, collect premiums, and settle claims—using tools like drones, satellite imagery, and mobile apps.

PPPs also enable financial literacy programs, digital enrollment processes, and better fraud detection mechanisms. They create a unified approach toward insurance inclusion, reduce administrative costs, and accelerate the adoption of technology-driven solutions such as e-KYC, telemedicine, and mobile claims processing.

As India seeks to increase insurance penetration, especially in rural and semi-urban areas, expanding and strengthening PPP models will be key. These collaborations ensure broader access, improve policy delivery, and support the national agenda of inclusive and sustainable insurance growth.

For Quick Revision

3.1 Growth Drivers of the Indian Insurance Sector

- Several socio-economic and policy factors are contributing to the steady growth of India's insurance market.

3.1.1 Increasing Financial Literacy and Awareness

- More people now understand the importance of risk management, savings, and investment. Awareness campaigns by the government and private insurers are helping individuals appreciate insurance as a tool for financial protection.

3.1.2 Government Push for Financial Inclusion

- Schemes like PMJDY and insurance coverage for the underserved have expanded the reach of insurance. Regulatory initiatives aim to make insurance accessible and affordable, especially in rural areas.

3.1.3 Rising Middle Class and Urbanization

- The expanding middle class, with higher disposable incomes, is driving demand for life, health, and asset insurance. Urbanization also promotes the adoption of insurance due to lifestyle-related risks.

3.1.4 Tax Benefits under Sections 80C and 10(10D)

- Insurance policies offer tax deductions on premiums paid (u/s 80C) and exemptions on maturity proceeds (u/s 10(10D)), encouraging individuals to invest in life insurance products.

3.2 Emerging Market Trends

- The insurance landscape is evolving with changing customer expectations and technological adoption.

3.2.1 Digital Transformation and Online Policy Servicing

- Online platforms allow policy purchase, renewal, and claim tracking through websites and apps, enhancing efficiency and transparency.

3.2.2 Demand for Personalized and Need-Based Policies

- Consumers seek plans customized to their life stage, profession, or health conditions, moving away from generic products.

3.2.3 Usage-Based and On-Demand Insurance Products

- Short-term and pay-as-you-use models (especially in auto insurance) are gaining popularity, particularly among millennials.

3.2.4 Growth in Term and Health Insurance Post-Pandemic

- The COVID-19 pandemic highlighted the importance of risk protection, leading to increased awareness and demand for term life and health insurance products.

3.3 Challenges in the Insurance Industry

- Despite growth, the sector faces several structural and operational issues.

3.3.1 Low Insurance Penetration and Awareness Gaps

- A large portion of the population remains uninsured due to limited understanding of insurance and lack of financial resources.

3.3.2 Delays in Claim Settlement and Trust Deficit

- Slow claims processing and poor customer service can reduce trust in insurers, deterring new customers.

3.3.3 Mis-selling and Lack of Transparency

- Agents sometimes sell unsuitable policies, leading to customer dissatisfaction and regulatory scrutiny.

3.3.4 Complex Regulatory and Compliance Burden

- Insurers must adhere to multiple regulations, which can delay innovation and increase operational costs.

3.4 Future Opportunities and Innovation Areas

- The sector is rapidly adapting to innovations and exploring underserved markets.

3.4.1 HealthTech and Digital Health Integration

- Wearables, telemedicine, and e-health records can be integrated with insurance to offer personalized premiums and wellness incentives.

3.4.2 Embedded Insurance

- Insurance is increasingly bundled with other products (e.g., smartphones, travel tickets), enabling seamless coverage and increasing penetration.

3.4.3 Artificial Intelligence and Predictive Analytics in Underwriting

- AI helps insurers assess risks more accurately, speed up underwriting, and detect fraud using data-driven insights.

3.4.4 Expansion into Tier II and III Cities and Rural Areas

- With urban markets reaching saturation, insurers are targeting smaller towns and rural regions with low-cost and need-based products.

3.5 Government Schemes and Their Market Impact

- Public initiatives have played a significant role in deepening insurance penetration.

3.5.1 Pradhan Mantri Jeevan Jyoti Bima Yojana (PMJJBY)

- A low-cost life insurance scheme offering ₹2 lakh coverage for an annual premium of ₹436, targeting low-income groups.

3.5.2 Pradhan Mantri Fasal Bima Yojana (PMFBY)

- Crop insurance aimed at protecting farmers from crop loss due to natural calamities, pests, or diseases.

3.5.3 Ayushman Bharat and Health Insurance Expansion

- India's flagship health protection mission provides free treatment coverage up to ₹5 lakh per family annually for low-income groups.

3.5.4 Role of Public-Private Partnerships in Insurance Access

- Collaborations between the government and private insurers help extend insurance benefits to remote and underserved areas efficiently.

Test Your Knowledge

2-Marks Questions

1. What is financial literacy in the context of insurance?
2. Mention any two government initiatives promoting financial inclusion.
3. How does urbanization impact insurance demand?
4. State any two tax benefits under Sections 80C and 10(10D).
5. What is online policy servicing?
6. Define need-based insurance products with an example.
7. What is usage-based insurance?
8. State one reason for the growth in health insurance post-pandemic.
9. Mention any two challenges leading to low insurance penetration.
10. What is meant by trust deficit in insurance services?
11. Define the term "mis-selling" in insurance.
12. Mention any two compliance-related challenges in the insurance sector.
13. What is HealthTech? Give one example.
14. Define embedded insurance with a suitable example.
15. What is the role of predictive analytics in insurance underwriting?
16. State any two reasons why insurers are focusing on Tier II and III cities.
17. What is PMJJBY? Who are its beneficiaries?
18. Name the crop insurance scheme launched by the Indian government.
19. What is the key objective of Ayushman Bharat?
20. Mention any two benefits of public-private partnerships in insurance.
21. What are personalized insurance policies?
22. List two innovations supporting insurance sector growth.
23. Write one benefit each of digital transformation for customers and insurers.
24. Mention two market trends observed after COVID-19 in the insurance sector.
25. Define "claim settlement delay" and give one possible reason for it.

5-Marks Questions

1. Discuss how increasing financial literacy and awareness are driving insurance penetration in India.

2. Analyze the role of government initiatives in expanding financial inclusion through insurance.
3. Examine the influence of the rising middle class and urbanization on insurance demand.
4. Explain the relevance of tax benefits under Sections 80C and 10(10D) in promoting life insurance products.
5. Evaluate the impact of digital transformation on customer experience in insurance servicing.
6. Analyze the rising demand for personalized and on-demand insurance products.
7. Explain usage-based insurance with examples. How does it benefit both insurers and customers?
8. Discuss how the COVID-19 pandemic influenced the growth of term and health insurance policies.
9. Examine the key reasons for low insurance penetration in India and suggest solutions.
10. Evaluate the effects of mis-selling and lack of transparency on consumer trust.
11. Discuss the regulatory and compliance challenges faced by insurers in India.
12. Analyze the role of HealthTech and digital health in transforming the insurance sector.
13. Explain embedded insurance and its potential in increasing policy adoption.
14. How is AI and predictive analytics reshaping underwriting and risk assessment?
15. Assess the market potential of Tier II and Tier III cities for insurance expansion
16. Describe the features and impact of PMJJBY and PMFBY on insurance coverage in India.
17. Analyze the role of Ayushman Bharat in boosting health insurance penetration.
18. Discuss the importance of public-private partnerships in improving insurance access.
19. Identify and explain two key future opportunities for innovation in the insurance industry.
20. Design an insurance outreach plan for rural India, incorporating digital tools, education, and government support.

About Author

Surjeet Kumar: A Life Dedicated to Learning and Inspiring Others

Surjeet Kumar's journey is an inspiring testament to the power of dedication and passion. Starting his teaching career right after finishing high school, he embarked on a path that transcended traditional expectations. His commitment to education not only nurtured young minds but also fueled his own intellectual growth. While excelling in academia, Kumar hasn't neglected his artistic side. His soul finds expression in poetry, with beautiful collections gracing the world. These verses likely touch upon the vast experiences gleaned from his dual roles as an educator and learner. And now, Kumar takes another remarkable step with the release of his second textbook. This latest offering signifies his willingness to share his accumulated knowledge and insights with a wider audience, impacting countless lives beyond the confines of
his classrooms.

www.ingramcontent.com/pod-product-compliance
Lightning Source LLC
LaVergne TN
LVHW082355200926
848481LV00012B/3572